Praise for *A Voice of Hope*

A Voice of Hope invites each reader to look within and discover the quiet presence of the mercy of God who longs to be known as the Beloved. The spiritual life is a way of living, loving and being in relationship with our God who offers us unconditional love and tender mercies. While you read, ponder, and reflect with Connie as a spiritual pilgrim along the way, be prepared to be met by God's loving embrace, and come to know that He dwells in you, through you, and upon you.

Reverend William J. Jarema, Author and Founder of Society of
Missionaries of Mercy, Mercy Center, Inc. (Colorado Springs, Colorado)

Connie's writing is beautiful and has a quality of drawing her readers in so they may walk with her and experience her fears, sorrows, and pain; even the grace of God. It is difficult to see those you know and love go through such trials as she describes, but it is also these same qualities that will speak in powerful ways to each one of her readers. For anyone dealing with Chronic Fatigue Syndrome (CFS), grief, depression, etc., this book is a powerfully empathetic voice. Connie speaks not only from her experience but also communicates God's grace, presence, and forgiveness in a way that others cannot. May God bless you, too, in your endeavors as you journey toward your own healing.

Reverend Harris Hoekwater, Senior Pastor
St. Joseph First United Methodist Church (St. Joseph, Michigan)

Connie's story is inspiring and will be a blessing to those who read it, whether they have had similar challenges in life or not. Even just the quotes she assembled are a great treasure. This book is also filled with Scripture and great reflection questions that can be a real help during a spiritual journey for anyone seeking God's power in their life.

Father Don Geyman, Sacramental Minister, Boyne Valley Catholic Community
Vocation Director, Diocese of Gaylord (Boyne City, Michigan)

Life is a journey and, like an education, it will have many commencements as you become enlightened. Connie's book can be a guide to finding your way and your destination.

Bernie Siegel, MD, Author, *The Art of Healing* and *A Book of Miracles*

A Voice of Hope is a sharing of faith. I was humbled by Connie's trust in me and in the Lord! I found her prayers and reflections all very moving and honest. I pray that you will continue to grow in your faith as we all continue on this journey with the Lord. May the Lord continue to bless and protect you!

Father Tony Judge, C.Ss.R., Redemptorist Missionary (Chicago, Illinois)

Connie's writings brought God's eyes, His hands, and genuine love for all His children to life. Many messages we need to hear are found in this book. Oftentimes, our sins and brokenness exist, because the devil has his clutches on all the goodness we seek. She inspires you to break free and travel a different road—not to the right or the left, but God says, *"Follow Me. I am always with you."* Connie's words convey God's messages, and they have touched my life!

Jane Webner, U. S. Army Veteran (Morrisville, North Carolina)

I applaud Connie's openness and honesty in dealing with the many struggles she encountered for so many years. This book will give courage to readers who are on a personal journey. The quotes complement each step of one's passage and discovery. The reflection questions helped me grow as a person, as a religious. May all who deal with depression, grief, setbacks, bad times, extreme fatigue, etc., find hope in reading Connie's memoir of struggle, trust, fortitude, and perseverance. Indeed her writings offer hope to those who may feel hopeless.

Barbara Hubeny, OP, Augustine Center (Conway, Michigan)

A Voice of Hope touched me at a time when I needed to hear there is hope after a rough journey of exhaustion. This book is a healing experience, and I couldn't put it down.

Theresa Jarema Hecker, St. Augustine Parishioner (Boyne Falls, Michigan)

These words reach my inner being with new meaning and thoughts each time I read and meditate on them. I've walked in Connie's shoes, and the further I get, the more I can relate. This book helps me release so many thoughts and feelings.

Lucille McHugh, Retired Office Staff (Vermilion, Ohio)

Connie reaffirms that, even in our lowest moments, God is always with us. We just need to let go, re-learn to pray, and most of all, listen. Like children, we begin to trust that God is by our side … always. Her reflections and questions reminded me to search my soul for more ways to be open to God in my life.

Anne Simms, St. Matthew Parishioner (Boyne City, Michigan)

Connie's story has captured the essence of God's love for us. Her book will encourage and help others discover their true spirit, regardless of religious affiliation. It shows readers how the Holy Spirit works through us and with us. *A Voice of Hope* is heartwarming, especially for those who struggle in life and tend to lose hope—it is proof that we are never alone in our suffering.

Martha Stanhope Dickhout, Spiritualist (Boyne City, Michigan)

Some people write what they think you should hear. Others write what they think sounds poetic; but Connie writes from her heart. Her reflections really made me search into my own heart.

Pat Klooster, Educator/Former Coach (Boyne City, Michigan)

A
VOICE of HOPE

A
VOICE of HOPE

A Spiritual Journey of Faith and Survival During
Overwhelming Grief, Depression, and Chronic Illness

CONNIE BRICKER SHALER

SHALER PUBLISHING
Boyne City, Michigan

All Bible quotes are from the Saint Joseph Edition of the New American Bible. Scripture texts in this work are taken from the New American Bible, revised edition © 1991, 1986, 1970 Confraternity of Christian Doctrine, Washington, D.C. and are used by permission of the copyright owner. All Rights Reserved. No part of the New American Bible may be reproduced in any form without permission in writing from the copyright owner.

"Blest Are They" by David Haas
Copyright © 1985 by GIA Publications, Inc. All rights reserved. Used by permission.

"Deep Within" by David Haas
Copyright © 1987 by GIA Publications, Inc. All rights reserved. Used by permission.

"Take Me Home" by David Haas
Copyright © 2001 by GIA Publications, Inc. All rights reserved. Used by permission.

"Voices That Challenge" by David Haas
Copyright © 1990 by GIA Publications, Inc. All rights reserved. Used by permission.

"With You By My Side" by David Haas
Copyright © 1998 by GIA Publications, Inc. All rights reserved. Used by permission.

"Without Seeing You" by David Haas
Copyright © 1993 by GIA Publications, Inc. All rights reserved. Used by permission.

"You Are Mine" by David Haas
Copyright © 1991 by GIA Publications, Inc. All rights reserved. Used by permission.

GIA Publications, Inc. 7404 S. Mason Ave., Chicago, IL 60638/www.giamusic.com 800.442.1358

Shaler, Connie Bricker.

    A voice of hope : a spiritual journey of faith and survival during overwhelming grief, depression, and chronic illness/Connie Bricker Shaler. —Boyne City, Michigan: Shaler Publishing, [2015]

       pages ; cm.

       ISBN: 978-0-9862242-2-5 (large print)
       ISBN: 978-0-9862242-1-8 (hardcover)
       ISBN: 978-0-9862242-0-1 (paperback)

1. Shaler, Connie Bricker. 2. Prayer—Christianity. 3. Christianity—Prayers and devotions. 4. Devotional exercises—Christianity. 5. Spiritual formation. 6. Healing—Religious aspects—Christianity. 7. Spiritual healing—Christianity. 8. Chronic fatigue syndrome—Treatment—Religious aspects—Christianity. 9. Chronic diseases—Treatment—Religious aspects—Christianity. 10. Mind and body therapies—Religious aspects—Christianity. 11. God (Christianity)—Love. 12. Private revelations. 13. Grief—Religious aspects—Christianity—Prayers and devotions. 14. Spiritual biography. 15. Prayers. I. Title.

       BT732 .S53 2015   2014920255
       261.8/321   1501

Printed and bound in the United States of America

COVER & TEXT DESIGN BY WWW.TOTHEPOINTSOLUTIONS.COM

In memory of my dearest, spiritual friend—
my first angel, Shirley Wuerth.

Dedicated to Shirley and to my family.

Contents

PART THREE: PRAYERS

PART FOUR: BLESSINGS

PART FIVE: ENCOURAGEMENT AND HOPE

PART SIX: IN HIS PRESENCE

PART SEVEN: END OF LIFE

AUTHOR'S NOTE

Throughout the book, wherever God, Jesus, or an angel is speaking, the text is italicized.

Preface

I n June 1986, God inspired me to write. From that point forward, nearly every time His words entered my consciousness, I wrote them down. While I searched for peace and contentment, His words and continued presence became my pathway, eventually leading me out of the darkness and breaking Satan's grasp on my soul.

God assured me time and again that He would always be with me, even when I felt abandoned. He encouraged me to trust Him by helping me understand my past. He longed for me to grasp the depth of His immense love and yearned for me to believe He held the answers to my questions and prayers. Once I was able to forgive myself, He urged me to move forward in my life.

Throughout my journey, God spoke directly to me and gave me signs. The first sign was from Jeremiah 30:1–2. "The following message came to Jeremiah from the LORD. Thus says the LORD, the God of Israel, *'Write all the words I have spoken to you in a book.'*" I heard His message spoken clearly and with authority!

The second sign came while I was listening to Lorna Kelly speak at a local church. After she read *Something Beautiful for God: The Classic Account of Mother Teresa's Journey into Compassion* by Malcolm Muggeridge, she was inspired to travel to Calcutta, India, to meet Mother Teresa. During Lorna's presentation, she shared stories about her relationship with Mother Teresa, as well as her own personal journey. Inside the front cover of Lorna's book, *The Camel Knows the Way*, in Mother Teresa's own handwriting, is: "Write that book for the Glory of God and the good of people." This phrase resounded over and over in my mind.

The third sign was in *Saint Faustina's Diary*. Jesus named Sister Mary Faustina Kowalska His private secretary. *"Your task is to write down everything that I make known to you about My Mercy, for the benefit of those who, by reading these things, will be comforted in their souls and will have the courage to approach Me."* I developed a deep spiritual connection with Saint Faustina as I continued to read incessantly. *"My secretary, write that I am more generous toward sinners than toward the just. It was for their sake that I came down from heaven; it was for their sake that My blood was spilled. Let them not fear to approach me; they are most in need of My mercy."* I, too, was most in need of Thy Mercy!

The fourth sign came from the book and movie titled *Conversations With God (CWG)* by Neale Donald Walsch. In the movie, God said, *"Have you had enough yet?"* and *"What are you waiting for?"* In another significant scene, Walsch walks into a room with a stack of legal pads, saying, "I started writing, and I couldn't stop." I have looked just like that—often carrying several yellow legal pads for months at a time, adding to them, and sharing what I had written. Not too long after watching the movie and reading Walsch's *CWG Trilogy*, I was browsing in a store in Boyne City (inspired living) and came upon a canvas hanging on the wall. **WHAT ARE YOU WAITING FOR?** – Lope de Vega. Okay, now God was sending me a sign in bold print!

The fifth sign came to me during a counseling session when I was advised to start writing in a prayer journal. I instantly recognized this as my fifth sign! At that point, I shared the four preceding signs, saying, "Now I know what I am supposed to do! I'm supposed to write a book!"

That very day, I shifted my focus and began the process. Nearly two years later, walking into the same office, I noticed a Bible open on a side table. There it was—Jeremiah 30:2, *"Write all the words I have spoken to you in a book"*—a repeat of the first sign, reaffirming that writing this book truly was what I was called to do.

So, how many signs did I need? Apparently, five—and two I received more than once.

What was I waiting for? I was not waiting any longer—and I began to answer His call to write this book *for the glory of God!*

Acknowledgments

I thank God for placing His words on my heart, in my conscious and unconscious thoughts, and revealing visions and dreams for me to remember. I thank God for being patient and placing His trust in me. I thank Him for each path He intended me to follow when I gained enough strength; when I decided I was ready, willing, and able. I thank God for granting me time to learn His lessons, so I could appreciate how I came to be at this point in my life and understand why. I thank God for deeming me worthy, granting me His forgiveness, allowing me to forgive myself. I am most thankful He helped me find the place within my heart and soul where He resides, knowing I could trust and believe in His incredible love for me.

To my husband, Frank, thank you for seeking me in the beginning and continuing to tell me how much you love me. Thank you for supporting me and enduring with me; caring about me and taking care of me, especially when I was sick, extremely fatigued, deeply depressed, and recovering. Thank you for waiting for me to find my way back, allowing me enough space that was essential for my survival. Thank you for being patient with me when I was broken, distant, and lost within myself. Thank you for allowing me enough time to work on this book, especially since God gave me clarity and placed urgency in my soul. Thank you for your loving, forgiving heart, devoting yourself to me in spite of it all! God truly blessed our lives when He chose you for me and me for you.

To our children, Michelle, Frank, and Becky, thank you for enduring and surviving my loss of health and so many boundaries it created within our family, especially when you were young. Thank you for your patience and being helpful whenever I needed someone close by. Thank you for understanding and showing compassion that gave me strength and hope, more than you will ever know. Since you have grown and moved on, thank you for continuing to be tender and considerate of my limitations, for still guarding me and being concerned, and always looking out for me! I love you all, and I am so proud of each of you. I also thank Stephen, Onica, and Rylan for loving my children, creating families you love, and sharing them with me! To our grandchildren, Aurora, Annabelle, and Ella; David, Zander, and Cannon; Jonah, Simon, and Abram—each of you brings incredible, loving joy into my heart and soul. All of you help me sustain a balance in my life, and I love you all so much!

To my brothers and sisters, my immediate and extended family, thank you for showing me what is important in life. Thank you for helping me become "who I am" today, believing in me, and encouraging me to never give up. Thank you for helping me see humor in simple things, making me laugh, even when I lost my ability and desire to smile—you helped me through it all. Thank you for your kindness, loving me as I was before and as I am now. I appreciate your insight and perspective, always being truthful and completely honest with me. I am most grateful your voices, laughter, and love live within me. I love you all back even more!

To Mark and Nancy Patrick, thank you for your understanding and loving support as I initially began to recover. Thank you for allowing me to care for Eric and Adam! Their presence brought joy back into my life and broke through my debilitating depression. Their innocence, love, and laughter helped facilitate my emotional and physical recovery. Thank you for sharing them with me and making a loving difference in my life. Thank you for allowing me to work for you and be a part of your lives—your belief and trust in me gave me self-confidence and a world of knowledge. When I was struggling to survive, you were always accommodating, allowing me whatever time I needed to recover. I can never thank you enough for your kindness, concern, and generosity. I am forever grateful!

To all my friends, hometown acquaintances, and faith community, you encouraged and helped inspire me by touching my heart and soul in loving ways. Your presence helped me survive and look to the future. Thank you for being in my life.

To everyone who read my manuscript before it was published, I am most grateful. I truly appreciate your willingness, time, and input that helped make this book possible.

A special thank you to Joyce Baker, a dear family friend, who initially entered my poems and writing into the computer.

To the staff of OfficeMax in Petoskey, thank you for your printing services prior to final publication. I appreciate your assistance and support of this book.

To my editor, Mary Jo Zazueta, your expertise and professionalism was amazing. Thank you for your patience and direction to bring *A Voice of Hope* to print! I appreciate your help through the process.

My sincere thanks to everyone who has touched my life and to those I will yet meet along the way—you are *my voice of hope*!

A
VOICE of HOPE

Introduction

I n July 1987, my health was suddenly compromised. My spirit was wounded. My soul was overtaken by sheer exhaustion. My body and mind had shutdown.

I awoke with severe abdominal cramping and soon realized I was unable to move, unable to speak. After being transported to the emergency room by ambulance, I was examined and then sent back home to rest. I slept and slept, and then slept even more. I slept around the clock, yet no relief. I couldn't sleep enough!

Days ran into nights, nights into days. For a long time, I couldn't do much of anything except sleep. My life was on hold, postponed for months and months, years and years. Time passed more slowly than you can imagine.

In the beginning, I was so weak it was a struggle just to breathe. To find a comfortable position to rest, without causing additional fatigue, was an effort. To change positions while lying in bed left me breathless. Before long, I slept in my recliner day and night in order to breathe and sleep easier. When I showered, I collapsed afterward; my energy was depleted. If any strength returned, I might get dressed, but I spent many days trying to be comfortable, trying to conserve what little energy I might have been granted that day.

It wasn't long before I realized I couldn't remember much of anything. If something was not written down, I would forget it. I often heard "I already told you. How could you forget? Do you know how many times you've asked? Don't you remember?" No, I couldn't remember.

The sounds of everyday life were overwhelming. I desperately wanted to continue being involved and connected with my family, but I couldn't endure noise. Everyday family interaction was more than I could tolerate most days. When overcome by too much sound, I would retreat to my bedroom, but I left the door open so I could hear what was going on from a distance. Many summer days, my children were taken to the beach so I could rest in peace and quiet.

Daylight was too bright, even inside our home. Blinds were pulled most of the time, and I often kept my eyes closed while awake to limit daylight. I never went outside without an umbrella to shield me from the brightness and warmth of the sun; it didn't matter what season of the year. Sunlight on my skin, but especially on my head, seemed to drain my strength even further in a very short time.

I searched for answers from many doctors, specialists, and psychologists, but only three actually believed I had a physical condition. Those who didn't know me personally or couldn't come up with a diagnosis suggested I was simply depressed, insinuating "it was all in my head."

Truly yearning to get well and be well, I willingly entered counseling. In my first session, the psychologist told me I needed to get rid of all the stress in my life. I wondered, what am I supposed to do with my husband and three kids? By our fourth session, he commented, "You need to be more assertive and aggressive in your health care. You need to stop letting doctors tell you, 'I think it's this, or you may have that,' and not give up until they find out what it is." He sincerely believed my fatigue was not psychological but had a physical cause. Realizing I could barely stay awake, he dismissed me early and released me from his care.

So, there I was. The psychologist said I wasn't depressed; it had to be something physical. Many doctors said it wasn't physical; it must be psychological. My MRI came back perfectly clear, ruling out a stroke, MS, and any other brain-type correlation. I continued to have blood tests when my symptoms changed, and I turned to additional specialists hoping to improve my health, hoping someone could diagnose this mysterious condition—yet there were no answers.

Out of anger and frustration, I tried to defy my fatigue. Disregarding how fragile I had become, I forced myself back to work after six weeks, since there was "nothing wrong with me." I was yet to realize that denying my body the rest it required would cause a deeper level of exhaustion. Pain began setting in and overtaking my body. While awake, sharp-and-piercing pain flashed throughout my body like lightning on the horizon. I felt like I had the flu for years on end; sometimes I felt like I had been beaten with a two-by-four. I was beginning to believe I had a body that only existed. I had lost all sense of pleasure and joy. I was barely hanging on and getting worse. By now I thought, who wouldn't be depressed?

Despair began to consume me. I continued to be considerably compromised and relapsing weeks on end was common. I shed tears of helplessness and disappointment, and I blamed myself. I was beginning to think I didn't deserve a better life. I had lost my ability to see beyond the present state my body and mind were in. I was blinded by pain and smothered by debilitating fatigue. My soul cried out for relief, longing for a glimmer of hope, but any hope of recovery seemed to be slipping away. Medical journal articles projected most Chronic Fatigue patients recovered somewhere between six months and two years—but two years had passed, and then five years came and went.

In and out of cognitive awareness was my new existence. It became difficult for me to differentiate between dreams and reality, unable to tell if I was asleep or awake, or was I stuck somewhere in between? When my fatigue was most merciless, dreams were more vivid and frightening. Reliving my initial episode was common, and upon awakening each subsequent time, I found myself unable to move, unable to speak.

As unrelenting fatigue continued to plague me, I could sleep anywhere, anytime. No matter where I was, I fell asleep—while stopped at a traffic light, standing up videotaping a basketball game, in the middle of a sentence while reading to grandchildren, and in the middle of conversations on the phone and in person. I would fall asleep shortly after waking up in the morning and after I had slept all day. For a while, I fell asleep nearly every time I sat down—during a brief visit at a friend's home, in doctors' waiting and examination rooms, during CAT scans and MRIs, in the dentist chair while having my teeth worked on, and in church on Sunday. Doing most anything exhausted me, doing nothing exhausted me.

Questions taunted and challenged my hope of recovery, leaving me to wonder if I would ever get better. Was this all I was going to have? Was this the way my life was going to be? Would any measure of strength or endurance return? If my fatigue subsided, would it be enough so I could have a functioning role within my family's home? Would my husband and children forgive me for not being able to contribute physically, to do what I had always done? Would they forget the times I felt I had let them down?

More than seven years passed before God began to present glimpses of hope while I was awake. He spoke to me more often, interjecting a word, a simple thought, or rhythmic sequence of phrases. Each time they entered my consciousness, I was compelled to write, sometimes several pieces a day.

Even though I felt God's presence more frequently, my soul remained deeply troubled. I still yearned and prayed for wisdom to understand, always longing for my health to improve, hoping I could reach a point where I would be able to maintain feeling well physically and mentally.

Before long, God began filling my mind with meaningful visions and dreams. "My Angel Came," "My Angel's Mission," and "The Kiss of My Angel" were inspired by the angels God sent. I saw "The Hand of God" interwoven in my life. I witnessed "Right to Life" during Mass–Jesus delivering a baby just before an abortion was going to take place. "Divine Vision" and "My Legacy" were significant visions that aided in healing my soul. Some dreams occurred numerous times, which allowed me additional opportunities to grasp what I needed to remember. They helped me understand what I couldn't comprehend when I was awake, giving me His hope to know my life could be different.

As I began seeking spiritual guidance, God revealed significant people who would lead me out of my despair, those He chose to help heal the wounds that were diminishing my existence. My minister's wife was the first who helped guide me. I sent her some of my poems, and her words of wisdom echoed within me: "You have a gift, but now you need to write about what you are thankful for. God has blessed you and your family. Show your gratitude by expressing what you believe and give Him thanks."

Taking her words to heart, my writing changed. A deeper spiritual essence evolved when I consciously considered what was good in my life, intentionally seeking and identifying what I was thankful for. I wrote about birth and life and life after death. I wrote about family and friends and those who became my blessings—regardless if they were angels helping guide me in a loving way or their presence was deliberately trying to destroy my soul. I wrote about the experience, wisdom, and knowledge I gained that gave me clarity and allowed me to believe with more conviction.

At times, I wrote day and night and while in prayer, asking God to find me worthy and heal my body, mind, and soul. I wrote about relinquishing all of my pain and heartache, trusting His will for my life. Upon accepting my surrender as complete and sincere, God blessed me with a promising sense of hope and peace of mind. I wrote about God and His people helping me understand, deepening my faith, and strengthening my soul.

My life changed before my eyes and I noticed my energy begin to increase. I learned to live within boundaries, for the most part, but I did test them often. Being able to stay awake all day, whether I did anything physical or not, was definitely an improvement. Eventually, I learned to discern the importance of my presence at an event or outing, weighing it against my vulnerability and risk of another relapse. Quite often, I'd spend most of the day resting to conserve enough energy to attend after-school functions.

As long as I avoided exertion, I discovered the spans of feeling well increased. Finally, ten years after my first episode, I felt as though my life was coming back. Even though my fatigue still seemed to wax and wane, it wasn't as severe. Life was good and getting better.

The pendulum continued to swing in times of trial, and I prayed asking God to save me from the challenge of Satan's warfare that was infiltrating my mind. In God's patient way, He continued to rescue me and battled Satan numerous times to protect me. Sometimes, I had to call out to God from the darkness of my soul; sometimes, He intentionally stepped forward and entered my consciousness, knowing I desperately needed reassurance and encouragement.

God continued being present in my life. He granted me desire, added endurance, and enough energy to persevere and trust Him even more. As dark as my life had been, God opened my eyes to see His light and helped me survive. He closed the abyss that separated me from Him, leading me on a journey out of darkness. He showed me I was worthy of His everlasting love, convincing me He was my hope and salvation.

Each time God came back to rescue me, He brought more loving and spiritual people into my life. He intervened when I felt desperate, abandoned, and forsaken. He knew I needed every person He sent, especially those who made a promising difference in my life. I also needed those who taught me lessons that were most painful, those who helped me clearly see the depth and contrast between good and evil.

In spite of everything I had been through, God acknowledged I still needed guidance and loving support, so He led me to a spiritual psychologist and spiritual director. They helped me work through my existing confusion and disturbance in my mind. They helped me find answers to questions I still had about my past, my faith, and my purpose in life. I followed their direction, and they helped me work through my deepest sense of loss. I began to read incessantly and believe with all my heart, that through Christ, there was hope for a better life!

The first book to help turn my life around was *The Search for Significance—We Can Build Our Self-Worth on Our Ability to Please Others or on the Love and Forgiveness of Jesus Christ* by Robert S. McGee. *The Dance of Intimacy, a Woman's Guide to Courageous Acts of Change in Key Relationships* and *The Dance of Anger, a Woman's Guide to Changing the Patterns of Intimate Relationships* by Harriet Lerner, Ph.D. were two books that brought reality and helped me identify feelings and understand relationships in a broader perspective. *The Angel Book, a Handbook for Aspiring Angels* by Karen Goldman opened my eyes to see angels and recognize their presence in my life.

As far as I had come, I was certainly not prepared for what hit me next: Satan's vindictive spiritual warfare. Whenever I began to regain strength and feel well, Satan waged another brutal attack on me, diligently trying to break me. He was unrelenting while placing specific people in my path who would cause me considerable pain. My faith was shaken, I was broken once again, and I was falling back into another incapacitating relapse. With each subsequent encounter, it was more difficult to endure. Satan knew exactly how to break my heart, how to crush and suffocate my soul. Even though I trusted in God, I was exhausted, defeated, and disappointed all over again. I tried to not question God's presence and protection, but I cried out and sought His strength and compassion, asking Him to spare me the pain He seemed to be allowing Satan to inflict on me.

For three long years, my life was completely out of control. The stability I longed for was out of my grasp. Whenever I tried denying I was severely depressed, my "crash" was more severe and traumatic than the last. At my worst, I truly thought I was losing my mind. I was ready to give up, believing my only hope to escape and make it all go away was to end my life and go Home. It took three years to determine I had a chemical imbalance, and then receive medications that stabilized my state of mind. It was such a relief to finally feel well.

Several more years passed while I continued to improve, but then, out of nowhere, as if the bottom fell out of my life, spiritual battles began all over again. As Satan continued to toy with me, taunting and torturing me like a cat playing with a mouse, I began losing my way. I felt I was slipping further and further from God's embrace. I was afraid I wouldn't survive another encounter with Satan, and I lived cautiously. I began to question and blame myself. I was angry because I "crashed" again. I was instantly caged inside my mind and I couldn't understand why. Why couldn't I get well and stay well? Why was God allowing this ongoing torment?

Even though I continued to seek and believe in God, I was struggling to not lose hope. Right then, God led me to read His Word, the *Bible*, cover to cover. By December 2009, it was *Souls in the Hands of a Tender God: Stories of the Search for Home and Healing on the Streets* by Craig Rennebohm with David Paul that helped make sense of my life. I was finally able to put enough pieces together and understand what happened on a deeper level, to understand how and why my body shutdown in 1987.

Quickly, God assembled my *Circle of Care*, a concept from Rennebohm and Paul's book, expanding it to include those who were capable of providing the professional care I desperately needed. I began to see my psychologist weekly, reading what I had written since my last appointment. And this time, God included a psychiatrist one or two times a week, because I was unquestioningly vulnerable and too unpredictable. I can't remember how many medication changes and adjustments occurred during that period of time, but I was closely monitored, and I felt safe in his care. I continued writing quite often, needing to clarify how I felt, describing the darkness, despondency, and fear that had overtaken me.

Together, they offered suggestions to help me see through the people Satan was using to blind and diminish me. In our sessions, their prayers and countless Scripture passages encouraged me to trust more in God's protection, reiterating I was worthy and precious in His eyes. They authenticated God's genuine love and respect for my progress. They helped facilitate my redefined identity, witnessing my honesty, sincerity, and renewed integrity. God promised I would survive, assuring me I would be safe with Him by my side.

As I relinquished fear of the intentions and deliberate acts Satan used to pierce my heart, I began to experience more explicit visions of love and mercy. I watched God protect me during the battles Satan continued to create within my soul. I walked with Jesus, and sometimes we were in the presence of God. An angel came and sat with me; she encouraged and reassured me. Many times God held me in His embrace, and sometimes I felt His presence and He talked to me. Inspiration and hope increased within me, and God diminished my pain, helping me endure the turmoil my soul continued wrestling with.

My health improved and my mind began to recover. Even though I was fragile and still didn't have much strength and endurance, I was living a better life than Satan led me to believe I deserved, a better life than he convinced me I was worthy of.

By the time I started to write this book, more than twenty-seven years had passed since by body first shut down. I don't understand why letting go of my heartache and struggle within my soul was so difficult, but Satan was so overpowering. Why had it been so hard to forgive those who caused me so much emotional pain? Why did it take me so many years to let go of those who broke me? At times, I couldn't understand why God had allowed Satan to push me so far.

Once I finally surrendered every person who hurt me, God granted me a keener instinct, helped redirect my vulnerability, and rebuilt my life. He showed me that someone's misplaced need for control and use of power over others was not Heaven sent. He taught me how to identify ulterior motives and when to question them, when to refuse to be submissive to people who abused their superiority, and when to take a stand. God also gave me enough strength and courage to walk away and trust Him, because "all this" was still part of His plan.

Through it all, God guided my thoughts and showed me how to pray for these people who had overstepped their bounds. In prayer, I began asking God to open their eyes so they could see their own sinful behavior, allowing them to ask for His forgiveness and mercy to save their own souls. Every time I recall their actions, I pray for them, and thank God for allowing me the same grace, love, and forgiveness.

In spite of all my pain and loss, I am thankful for times of silence and feeling abandoned, for each bout of spiritual warfare, feeling inferior and forsaken. I learned to give thanks each time Satan had intentionally abused me, each time I was in grips of unrelenting anguish, each time Satan managed to defeat me once again.

I am thankful I found unconditional love in the arms of God. I am thankful for His forgiveness of my sins, and most thankful He never lost hope in me. I was blessed every time He came back to rescue me, every time He fought for my soul, every time He protected me from harm. I am thankful for everything and everyone who has helped me become who I am today. God blessed me with specific people, angels, and visions, and I am so grateful He chose them to help me survive in this life.

Lastly, I am thankful for God's presence, especially when I hear His voice ... *a voice of hope*!

"No trial has come to you but what is human. God is faithful and will not let you be tried beyond your strength; but with the trial, he will also provide a way out, so that you will be able to bear it."
—I Corinthians 10:13

"If we live our lives as a gift, it is possible to reach a blissful state of eternal happiness. Know that every breath is a miracle and every moment a blessing, and you will achieve your dreams."
—Micheal Teal, *The Ancient One*

REFLECTION

I would not have survived to this point in my life without Divine Intervention, because I was so broken and so close to giving up. God and the people He sent saved me from myself and from evil in this world more than once. These godly people have blessed me, but I owe my life to Him!

PART ONE

He Speaks to Me

"Do not be afraid, I am with you …
I have called you each by name.
Come and follow me; I will bring you home.
I love you and you are mine!"

DAVID HAAS, *You Are Mine*

I Know

I know you want to have control of things in your life,
but I have everything in control—you can trust Me.
I know you are afraid and don't know what to expect,
but I have a plan and already know the outcome.

I know you are broken and things in this life have hurt you,
but I can heal your brokenness and take your pain away.
I know you feel you are amidst a battle you'll never win,
but the battle is not yours—I already fought and won it for you.

I know you are tired and weary,
but I will give you strength to persevere.
I know you want to be at peace,
but I am the peace you seek.

I know you feel helpless and sometimes hopeless,
but I can help you—I am your hope for this world.
I know you are seeking and longing for so much more in this life,
but I am what you seek—I am the one you long for.

I know you are disappointed in things you have done or failed to do,
but I have forgiven you and given you a new life.
I know you feel unworthy of being loved,
but you are worthy—I love you with all My heart.

I know you feel lost in the darkness of this world,
but I am the light to show you the way.
I know you hope to be with Me one day,
but I have never left your side.

I know you are discouraged and feel you have no place to call home,
but this is part of your journey, and I have prepared a place for you.
I know you are concerned and worried about your future,
but you will be okay—I've got this.

"Everything indeed is for you, so that the grace bestowed in abundance on more and more people may cause the thanksgiving to overflow for the glory of God. Therefore, we are not discouraged; rather, although our outer self is wasting away, our inner self is being renewed day by day."
—II Corinthians 4:13–16

"Without mercy, our darkness would plunge us into despair; for some, self-destruction. Time alone with God reveals the unfathomable depths of the poverty of the spirit. We are so poor that even our poverty is not our own: It belongs to the mysterium tremendum of a loving God."
—Brennan Manning, *The Ragamuffin Gospel:*
Good News for the Bedraggled, Beat-Up, and Burnt Out

REFLECTION

In 2012, I attended a Women's Retreat at Cran-Hill Ranch in Michigan. Karen Hossink, speaker and author, closed her presentation by suggesting "Couch Time with GOD." While I cleared my mind, God began to speak to me. He understood everything I longed for, everything I struggled with, every time I fell into depression. I realized my life had become too busy and overwhelming. I was too exhausted and screaming so loud on the inside, I couldn't hear Him. God whispered His words of encouragement and waited patiently for me to be still and seek His guidance. He longed for me to feel His presence and find rest in His embrace.

Do you believe God knows everything in your heart? Has He helped you find words to express yourself?

Whatever is troublesome or unresolved, do you believe God understands you? Has God helped you understand yourself?

A Vision

Jesus held my hand last night
and led me down a path of white.
Time stood still as we strolled on ahead …
past unearthly wonders—God's heavenly end.

He stopped and then smiled, as He turned toward me,
"I died for your sins … to set you free!"
As greater brightness surrounded us there,
He healed my heart and removed my fear.

His reassuring presence calmed my restless, yearning soul,
then He forgave me all my sins; my emptiness, now full.
Quiet, simple contentedness and absence of all pain,
He relieved discomfort from within; His promise He sustained.

He indulged me with peace of mind, showing me His blessings.
Together, we stood with God amidst His gifts of grace unceasing.
He led me to a few I loved—Dad, Aunt Pat, and John—
it seemed we talked forever, then Jesus said, *"Come on.*

"In good time, you will return, but now it's time to go.
I wanted you to see a glimpse of your future Heavenly Home!"

"Then the LORD came down in the column of cloud, and standing at the entrance of the tent, called Aaron and Miriam. When both came forward, he said, 'Now listen to the words of the LORD: Should there be a prophet among you, in visions will I reveal myself to him; in dreams will I speak to him; not so with my servant Moses! Throughout my house, he bears my trust: face to face I speak to him, plainly and not in riddles. The presence of the LORD he beholds.'"
—Numbers 12:5–8

"To come to the unconscious as a supplicant desiring wholeness puts us in the right attitude to find inner healing. Then we can find the help from within that comes from recalling dreams, seeking to understand them, and relating to their potential for wholeness."
—John A. Sanford, *Dreams and Healing*

REFLECTION

"A Vision" was one of the first visions I was able to recall and write down. It gave me a calming sense of peace, reaffirmed my belief in life ever after, and reassured me, that even in death, God still has a plan for us to be reunited with those we love.

Has God or Jesus come to you in a vision or a dream? Did He reveal wisdom or give you a conscious awareness? Were His words healing or comforting? Did He give you hope?

If you had a vision, have you shared it with someone? Did they help you see symbolism and parallels to relate to your life experience? Did your vision change your outlook on life or death?

My Angel Came

My angel came and said, *"It's time."*
And there she stayed right by my side.
She held me close while in her arms—
her soft, gentle smile now eased my mind.

"No need to fear!
You won't be alone.
I will always be with you.
It's time to come Home!"

"But I'm so young, and I want to stay!
I'll miss Mom and Dad!
They'll miss me every day!"

"No need to fear! I know they'll miss you,
I understand, and in time, they will, too.
You've no need to worry,
they will all make it through.
You will be happy once you arrive,
and most exciting of all, with God, you're alive!
He is loving and kind, and He loves us all!
He loves little children and the young most of all!
At times, Mom and Dad won't think of you as gone.
You're always in their hearts and on their minds!"

I simply sat there, pondering what to do,
but I knew she was right—to be with God, I had to!

"So you see, Mom and Dad, I love you a lot!
I want you to be happy, and you need fear not!
To my family and friends, and everyone so dear,
think of our good times and His joy I've found here!
Even though I miss you and wish you were here,
remember I'll still love you more and more each year!
My angel came!"

"... 'cause there will be a time when I'll see your face, and I'll hear your voice, and there, we will laugh again. And there will come a day when I'll hold you close, no more tears to cry ... 'cause we'll have forever, but I'll say goodbye for now."
—Kathy Troccoli, "Goodbye for Now"

REFLECTION

While attending the funeral of a young girl, I saw an angel come and stay at her side. Her angel spoke, letting her know her parents were going to be okay. God blessed me with this vision—to see the angel He sent and to hear the angel's words of hope and reassurance. Thanks be to God!

Have you or someone close to you experienced a tragic death? Can you envision God sending someone, an angel or Jesus, to be with your loved one and take him or her Home?

Can you envision the same for yourself—an angel, God, or Jesus coming to be with you as you try to survive your loss and devastation? Can you let them into your heart to comfort you? Can you feel them lifting your sorrow and grief as they tell you, *"It's going to be okay"*?

God's Challenge

D on't listen to the voices of the world that diminish you. Challenge those voices with My Word, the Word of God. Listen for My voice. I will encourage you. I will lift you up. I will only tell you the Truth.

Stop trying to fit into this world; it is only temporary. Challenge yourself to find Me. Follow My people and My ways. Use the gifts I've blessed you with to seek and discover My purpose for your life. Once you do, you will also find your passion.

Don't take yourself so seriously. Challenge yourself to allow Me to ease what weighs you down. Laugh with Me. Let Me renew your life with hope and joy. Seek people who are filled with laughter, and look in the mirror. They will help increase your joy and lighten up your life.

Stop surrendering to this world and getting lost. Challenge yourself to surrender only to Me. Have courage and seek Me in every challenge you face. Follow Me and I will protect you and fight battles for you. Battles of this day are not yours—they are between Satan and Me, and I will always win. With Me, you will never lose.

Don't allow yourself to be bound by anxiety or desperation. Challenge yourself to release their hold on you. Reevaluate everything that burdens your life. Allow Me to calm your soul. I will fulfill your needs, ease your pain, and grant you peace of mind.

Stop giving up on yourself and forgetting who you are. Challenge yourself to persevere and ask for My strength to endure. Seek My answers to understand; ask for My knowledge to gain wisdom; seek My Word for encouragement. I believe in you—believe in Me—believe in yourself.

Don't try to hide your pain with unhealthy behavior. Challenge yourself to live in spite of your pain, in spite of your heartache and disappointments. Accept what life deals you as a pathway that leads you closer to Me. I will give you everything you need to fulfill My plans for your life.

Stop thinking you have been deserted. Challenge yourself to believe you will never be alone again, because I will never leave you alone to suffer. I am right by your side; I am here when you don't think of Me or ask for Me. I am here even when you think you want to blame Me, even when you are disappointed with Me. When you feel I've let you down, when you think I do not hear your prayers, it means not yet. I have something greater planned for you.

Don't try to go through this life alone—you need people, you need Me. Challenge yourself to let Me sit with you and embrace you. Accept My open arms and embrace Me back. When I reach out for you, you need to take My hand. I will walk through dark valleys with you, and I will carry you whenever you are too weak for your journey. You will never be alone again.

Stop letting go of Me, thinking I have abandoned or forsaken you. Challenge yourself to hold onto Me and never let go! There may come a time when you will think you can live without me, but you will have been deceived. I will hold onto you forever, and I will not let you fall! I created you to live with Me in Eternity.

Don't be afraid of what is to come—I know the rest of the story. Challenge yourself to continue onward through changes and trials in your life. I will help you through the lessons you need to learn, because some will be difficult. You will experience miracles and tragedies, you will love and grieve, but it's worth every moment! I have given you free will, so it is your choice to be happy or sad, to be joyful or miserable. I want you to have a joyful life here and now,, and then come and live with Me in Paradise. I promise, you will have a better life, if you trust and believe in Me!

"There are times in every person's life, when you feel you can't go on ... when each step hurts and feels like a mile and your peace and joy are gone. It's then you must realize deep inside if you want to make it Home. You must yield your heart and depend on God! You are loved and not alone! For it is in the yielding and surrender, and the life lessons you learn ... that even though broken, when you dwell in Christ, your joy and peace will return! If you are fighting depression, hold on to God ... there is hope!"

—Elizabeth Holowasko, Ordained Minister,
Pentecostal Church of God, *Facebook posting 04/23/12*

REFLECTION

God demanded Satan to let go of me, but Satan refused. Instead, Satan *stepped up his game* to crush and destroy me once and for all. Satan and his followers continued to confront and taunt me; they became fierce, vicious, and relentless.

God loved me as His Beloved, and He knew I needed Him more than ever. Since Satan hated me more than you could imagine, God stood guard over me with His mighty armor, shielding my heart and soul from further pain and harm. To protect me, God overturned tables of evil so I could no longer see or hear their wickedness. God challenged me to listen and obey His Words, to trust and believe in His power, to surrender and accept His promise to save my soul!

Has Satan tempted you, maybe even helped you justify what you truly knew was wrong in your heart? Have you ever believed Satan's lies, feeling as though someone had done you wrong, so it was okay for you to hurt them the way they hurt you? What was the outcome, and what did you learn?

Have you found God challenging you to listen only to Him? Have you always obeyed, or have you been humbled and learned what God wanted you to know the hard way? Do you believe God wants you to have an easier or better life, a life of happiness, peace, and joy? If not, why?

Know That I Am

I created you because I have a plan for you in this lifetime. You are My chosen people—beautifully made, perfect and unique, an absolute blessing in My eyes! Accept Me into your life, and believe I am here to save you! You can trust My Word and rest in My embrace!

My enduring dream for you is to be able to feel secure in My world, knowing Heaven awaits your arrival. I long for you to experience true love—genuine and sincere, deeply committed, and unquestionably heart-felt! I loved you before you were born; I always have and I always will! On Earth, as it is in Heaven, My love for you is everlasting; My love is boundless and unconditional; My love is eternal!

Before you were conceived, I had an unwavering hope for you to make a difference in this lifetime. Upon you I bestowed pure and refined talents and gifts, anticipating you would share them with those you love and those in need.

You are amazing! Remember your goodness! I know your heart and all that you long for—especially when you feel you have lost yourself. I know every personal inner battle you encounter, and I know when you feel your life is out of control, when you feel defeated and broken.

Here on Earth, I witness every moment. I see your struggles when you are being challenged; I see what causes you to begin to question yourself. I feel the intensity of your pain and anguish, and I weep with you. When I watch you sacrifice your soul, I see how desperate you are to understand your inner conflict and discover what is missing. I am always right here, hoping you will turn your life back around and seek Me.

I know some of your choices have wounded you deeply, and My heart breaks for you. I observe your great sadness knowing you are still disappointed in yourself for the times you had compromised what you believed. I know about the times you actually knew in your heart what I desired for you, but you were hoping you might grasp what you felt you needed to survive. I felt your distress when you knew you forfeited your self-respect, *hurting not only yourself, but also those you loved the most. I have observed how self-destructive you have been, and I also see the damage it causes.*

I can hardly bear waiting for you to surrender your old ways, but I am patient, and I want to renew My Covenant with you. I want to guide your heart and help you fulfill your commitment to live a better life, to know you are entitled to a better life!

When you're so exhausted and think your life is beyond hope, seek Me and allow My words of wisdom to comfort you and give you rest! Listen and hear what I have to say, as well as words spoken by those who follow Me, those who know and trust in My ways. Listen when they share their own life stories. You will know who they are by the truth they speak. They will offer insight to help you find your way back by helping you recover and restore faith in yourself and Me. They will help you acquire a Heavenly peace of mind to believe and trust in My Divine Mercy! Stand down and allow us to help you!

When you decide you are ready to come before Me and acknowledge your sinfulness, My heart will leap for joy! When I hear you say, "I am so sorry," I will have already forgiven you. Over time, those who love you will learn to forgive you, too. My continuous prayer is I hope you will allow Me to ignite the passion you need to live your life as I intended you to live! I understand your shame and disappointment; I understand your anger and rage, but I will also help you work through it. I am the only one who can wipe your sins away and remember them no more.

I did not create you with the intent you must struggle and have to figure out this life by yourself. I never intended your life to be so difficult. I had hoped you would have made other choices, but I do not blame you. I want to bless you and fulfill your heart and soul's desire, but I will wait until it is your choice, until you are ready to surrender! No matter what has happened, if it was only once, or even if it was numerous times, continue to return to Me. When you are most devastated, I will embrace you and save you every time.

When you wish you would just stop breathing, I will breathe My life into you. I will inspire you to breathe again and again, because it is in My power to decide when you will breathe your last breath. Seek Me when your life is so bad you have lost hope.

When you strayed, I understood why your decisions took you where they did. I observed each time you sought the unconditional love you desperately long for. Whenever your world came crashing down around you, I tried to save you, but I couldn't save you from yourself until you decided you had enough. I want to hold you close and soothe your pain. I want to calm your disturbed sense of being and help you know it is not the end of the world!

You can trust Me when I show you people are not who they appear to be. You will be able see their ulterior intentions, and I will protect you from their self-claimed power when they insist they have a right to control you or 'lord' over you. I will diminish their joy when they try to intentionally hurt you. I will take their breath away and the wind out of their sails when they lash out and you are their target. I will shield your heart and soul from their destruction.

I long for you to forgive yourself and those who hurt you. I hope and pray you will learn to let it all go. I want you to surrender all that burdens your heart and soul, and hand it over to Me. I am your hope when your life is so difficult, especially when you think you won't survive the battle. I will save you and protect you from those who are determined to battle against you.

Seek Me when your life is in or out of control. I will help you and always allow you to express yourself, to find the words you have buried and suppressed for so long. I will help you be able to release your discouragement and sadness; I will help you discover the answers you need. Whenever you are extremely depressed, during times of your most intense grief and sorrow, I am here to free your soul from the grips of Satan. I will release you from his cage of darkness.

I will remind you of your vows and commitments, and I pray you will not give up on each other! Through it all, I believe you know how much you need Me, but you aren't ready to release the reins. Deep down, I can see you are still hoping you can 'pull this off' or 'get it together' by yourself. It is not a sign of weakness if you feel you have failed; it is a sign of surrendering what is out of your grasp.

So, here you are and here I am! I want you to have the simplest things in life—a life filled with Divine joy, Heavenly peace, and an unwavering faith and trust in Me! I see your progress, learning what I have required you to learn. I smile upon you throughout the day and night, enjoying what I see as I witness your eagerness and thirst for understanding life! I admire your immense capacity for kindness and compassion for others; by showing concern for each one; by giving your time, attention, and love to all My people; and loving Me!

If you should begin to think you have faltered or question anything in your life, just turn to Me! Ask and I will help you see things in a new light. I want to show you what a difference I can make in your life and what a difference you are making in the lives of others!

Whether you can see to find Me through the darkness of night or you are blinded by the brightness of day, I am here! I have always said, "Ask and you shall receive," but I will wait until you are ready to ask. I know you will find your way. I know you are capable of anything you put your mind to, especially when you know it is the right thing to do!

These things you need to remember: You are not alone. I am in the silence, stillness, and darkness. You will find Me wherever you are, whenever you seek Me! I am in your presence and enduring your trials with you, feeling everything you feel! Allow My embrace to surround and protect you, to guide and sustain you! I admire your conviction and I will help you survive when you place your trust in Me!

Know that I am, always and forever, your God!

"Jesus is living next to you, in the brothers and sisters with whom you share your daily existence. His visage is that of the poorest, of the marginalized ... Jesus' dwelling is wherever a human person is suffering because rights are being denied, hopes betrayed, anxieties ignored. There in the midst of humankind is the dwelling of Christ, who asks you to dry every tear in His name, and to remind whoever feels lonely that no one whose hope is placed in Christ is ever alone."

—Pope John Paul II,
compiled by Mary Emmanuel Alves and Molly H. Rosa,
Spiritual Advice from John Paul II

"God never forces Himself upon us or works in us beyond what we are willing to allow Him to do. If we do not grow in love, it is not because His love for us is limited, but because we set limits to what His love can do in us."

—Thomas Green, *When the Well Runs Dry*

REFLECTION

God spoke to me, reminding me of everything I already knew, but I seemed to keep forgetting. During my darkest times, God came back to save me, reassure me, and convince me I was still worthy. In the darkness I was so lonely, but God never left my side. He kept speaking out to reach me, hoping I would hear His voice!

Do you sometimes forget what God truly wants for you? Have you ever come to a crossroad and didn't know what to do? Were you ever at a point in your life when you knew God's will, but you weren't quite ready to do it? Were you afraid? Do you know why you were hesitant?

Are you truly satisfied with your life and the condition of your soul? Are you at peace? Why or why not? If you could, what would you change today about your life?

A Letter from Jesus to a Young Man

My Dearest One,

I hold you up, because I love you! I will support you with My strength, because My arms will not grow tired or weary—I will never let you fall. I will carry you as long as it takes, because I want you to be able to walk beside Me, strong and tall. I pray for the day you will turn and face Me, man-to-man, embracing your Brother and loving Father!

I know you want a better life. I know you wish your life would be easier, because you have struggled so many years wishing it were different. I understand all that burdens your heart and grieves your soul. I know when and why you stopped believing in Me, even though you may not fully understand it yet. I am always listening, so speak until you have spoken all that troubles you, especially when you want to blame Me, especially when you think I don't even exist anymore. Give unto Me your sorrow and sadness; hand over your frustrations, fear, and despair. Once you begin to release them, I will be able to ease your pain and replace it with healing and gratitude.

I know you are discouraged. I know you still think you should be able to carry your cross alone, but how many times do you think you need to fall before you allow Me to help you or carry it for you? I couldn't carry My cross, because it was more than I could bear, so do not be ashamed or think of this as a weakness. I have watched you stumble every step of the way, determined you will not give up or give in. Your life could be easier if only you would let go, and let My presence return your strength and belief in a better tomorrow!

I have noticed when you are disappointed in others and how it tortures you. For all those times when someone sinned against you, did you wrong, or broke your heart, possibly without knowing, all you need to do is turn to Me. I will help you forgive them … this alone will change your life.

Since I gave you free will, it is your choice to decide when you are ready to move on in your life. Whenever that is for you, call out My name. Confess your sins. You can believe in Our Heavenly Father's forgiveness. He is a loving God, and you can trust in Me. Don't you remember—I died on the cross to free you from sin? I did not want you to suffer as I did, even though it was nearly two thousand years ago, and I still love you that much.

Whenever you need to, cry until there are no more tears. It shows Me the depth of how much you care, how much you have loved, and how much you love now. May your tears of sadness turn to joy and fill your heart and soul until it overflows with goodness.

I am always in your presence, but sometimes I will be silent and wait for you to notice Me. I may whisper your name and nudge you, or I will call out your name and beckon you. Depending on your vulnerability and state of mind, I may give My voice and message to someone who can get through to you, but I will not cease trying to reach you. You can believe in My words because I only speak words of Truth. Once you open your heart and soul, My words will become your words of Truth. One day, you will use them to touch someone else who needs Me, and they will find Me through you!

Allow Me to reenter your life; allow Me to rescue you. With Me, you shall find comfort and peace of mind, and an incredible sense of fulfillment will exceed your greatest imaginings. Nothing you ever seek will fully satisfy your desires and longing like My presence within you. I know you know I Am the One!

Like you, I, too, am a child of God. You are My brother, and I will never forsake you. I pray for you like everyone should pray for his or her own family. Have courage and know in your heart I believe in you no matter what happens. I can turn everything into a most loving outcome, even your life. I have a plan for you, and I already know your future!

May the work of your hands become a labor of love and evolve to show the love of God lives in your heart. Remember, My earthly father was a carpenter, too. Make use of the talent God gifted you with, and make Us proud of your handiwork. You were chosen to develop it into your passion, using it in countless loving ways, blessing your life when sharing your gifts with others.

Breathe in the Spirit of My love. Let the fire of My soul warm you and restore loving kindness in your heart. May its glowing light lead you back to My salvation, so you can see to find your way and know you are on the right path.

In My embrace, may the beating of My heart calm your restlessness and return rhythm and certainty to your life. May My life-giving water refresh you, nourish you, and cleanse you; may it heal your wounded and broken existence.

I pray for a miracle in your heart, so your faith and trust in Me will be restored. May the love of Our Father satisfy your longing heart so you may discover your significance here and now!

Always remember, I will never give up on you, I will always love you, and My love is the greatest love you will ever know!

Living in God's eternal love, Jesus

"The Lord is the everlasting God, the Creator of the ends of the earth. He will not grow tired or weary, and his understanding, no one can fathom. He gives strength to the weary and increases the power of the weak."
—Isaiah 40:18–31

"Jesus did not come to explain away suffering or to remove it. He came to fill it with His presence."
—Paul Claudel, *A Friar's Life*

REFLECTION

In *Forgiven*, a painting by Thomas Blackshear II, Jesus is robed in white, supporting the broken body and soul of a young man, His arms wrapped under the man's arms and around his chest. Turned away from Jesus and unable to stand on his own, the young man holds a mallet and spikes, like the ones used to nail our Savior to the cross. The young man's head hangs low in shame while Jesus embraces his weakened body and spirit. Jesus spoke these words of encouragement and hope—directing this man to listen and do as He commanded him to do—to accept healing and forgiveness while being held in His arms. When I saw this framed painting for the first time, my emotions swept me away. I was caught in a torrent of feeling unworthy, undeserving, and ashamed of things I had done in the past. Tears of sadness beckoned for a relationship of acceptance, unconditional love, and total forgiveness.

If your spirit is broken, whether you are a man or a woman, envision Jesus in your presence. If Jesus wrote you a letter today, what would He tell you?

Write Jesus a letter and tell Him what you want Him to know about you. Explain what you are going through, tell Him what causes your struggle and inner turmoil, and let Him know what you are afraid of. Ask Him whatever questions you need answered, and wait for His response. No matter how long it takes, write it down.

May you be blessed with answers and the encouragement you are seeking! May you open your heart to accept what God feels you need at this time.

Jesus Rescued Me

I had managed to break away from being entrapped in the snare of Satan's follower, but the devil himself continued to torment my conscious existence. Satan insidiously intended to destroy all hope for the life and love I longed for. Whenever I envisioned thoughts of a better life, he chanted words and phrases that penetrated and pierced my heart and mind like swords.

Satan planned to bring further harm to my family and me, to separate me from them, and to isolate me from a life with God. I seemed unable to defend myself, as if I had no shield or sword—Satan confiscated those in my mind to diminish my ability to fight him off. He blinded me so I could not see him or have a fighting chance of survival, so he could mock and ridicule me before his followers. His conniving manner and maliciousness was haunting, convincing me and everyone else I was unworthy. He would see to it that no one would ever want me, love me, or forgive me—not even God.

Satan succeeded and pushed me over the edge into his darkened, frightening abyss. Buried far beneath the depths of my despair, devastated and broken, Satan reveled in causing me to believe I didn't deserve any better, to believe I had been abandoned, to believe I would live the rest of my life alone.

I managed to block out Satan's taunting echo for a while, but I couldn't endure it any longer, and I couldn't figure out how to make him stop. Already hidden in the shame of Satan's abyss, I had no way to escape, nowhere to go. I wanted to completely vanish, to disappear forever! In my last and final hope, I cried and screamed out from the depths of my soul, "God, please save me from Satan's torture. You are my only hope!"

In that very moment, Jesus came to rescue me. He found me in the farthest edge of my darkness, and His light brought me immediate warmth and compassion, shielding me from Satan and his people's devious intentions.

Jesus looked at me lovingly, tenderly gazing into my heart and soul, but I turned away, trying to hold back my tears. I was extremely embarrassed and so sorry, since I realized I had sacrificed my soul while searching for the unconditional love my heart desperately longed for. The weight of my shame smothered me, choking my ability to breathe as it welled up in my throat.

Jesus reached out and turned my head toward Him, sustaining His ever-loving gaze on me. He cupped my face in His hands and waited patiently for our eyes to meet. In His soft-spoken and nurturing voice, He asked, *"Why can't you let it all go?"*

I hesitated and sighed deeply before I had enough courage to look directly into Jesus's eyes once again. A river of tears streamed down my face, and I sobbed uncontrollably as I began releasing every disappointment I had in myself. My heart broke open and a downpour of grief, misery, and hopelessness was totally exposed before Him.

As we began examining my soul, God showed me how my profound sorrow and shame had caused my overwhelming sadness. He replayed visions from my past, allowing me to vividly see in His light, allowing me to remember every circumstance that led to the sacrifice of my body and soul. He never once questioned my thoughts or actions, but gradually and subtly, He revealed each underlying issue that seemed to separate me from His love.

Time and again, He exposed His presence throughout my life, so I could recognize Him in others. He showed me when He tried to protect me. He showed me when I turned Him away and refused Him. He showed me specific times in my life when I was still under the insidious spell of Satan and I could not see through his evil ways.

In that moment, I began to collapse, but Jesus clutched my weakened body. With ease, He lifted me into His arms like a bridegroom carrying his bride. I felt secure and safe, and His mighty, loving embrace was wondrous. His immense concern for my well-being consoled me. His whispers calmed my anxious and exhausted broken spirit.

Jesus continued assuring me, *"I never intended for you to be tortured by Satan's wrath. You are going to be okay. Remember, I am only a touch and breath away. I will never forsake you; I am here to protect you, save you, and take care of you. I will help you recover and regain your strength. My power and mercy will heal you!*

"You need to totally surrender everything! Allow Me to erase memories that have caused you so much heartache and grief. I will bestow upon you an ability to feel My presence every moment of your life! I promise I will remain in the forefront of your consciousness. I will not allow you to ever feel as though I have left you.

"As soon as you can let go of your past long enough to allow Me to work miracles in your life, I will replace your pain with My abounding love! Your eyes will be opened, and you will be able to see what is good in your life. I will show you glorious wonders, and you will experience glimpses of Heaven on Earth, as well as life in Eternity! My Spirit has found a dwelling place within you, to guide and protect you all the days of your life! You will never have to doubt My love for you. You will know with certainty I have forgiven and forgotten all your sins. Always and forever, I am the unconditional love you seek!"

I felt fixated in Jesus's arms, and my sighs grew deeper, returning my breathing to normal. I felt the beat of His heart, the rise and fall of His chest. I felt my soul absorbing His love, and His healing power being infused throughout my body.

Drifting off into an entranced realm, but unable to move or speak, God allowed me to watch as He battled Satan and his followers. He pinned their evil ways under His foot, forcing them to release their bondage. God silenced their evil lies and wicked torment they had used against me when they caged my soul. I winced when I heard Satan's wailing rage as God withdrew me from their clutches, pronouncing, *"She is My Beloved!"* God cursed them, demanding they all turn away and remove me from their target once and for all!

Only a moment passed before Jesus stirred me, and I instantly knew my faith and health had been restored. He wept with me, reminding me to always offer prayers of thanksgiving, giving glory to God, Our Father. He looked intently into my eyes once again, saying, *"I sacrificed My life for you, because I do love you that much! You are My Beloved! You are God's Beloved Daughter! Rest for now, then follow Us!"*

⌇

"There is no honest way to explain it, because the only people who really know where it is are the ones who have gone over."
—Hunter S. Thompson, *The Edge*

"Our brokenness is God's pain. Every tear we shed becomes His tear. He may not yet wipe them away, but He makes them His. Would we rather have our own dry eyes, or His tear-filled ones? He came. He is here. That is the salient fact. If He does not heal all our broken bones and loves and lives now, He comes into them and is broken, like bread, and we are nourished. And He shows us we can henceforth use our very brokenness as nourishment for those we love. Since we are His body, we too are the bread that is broken for others. Our very failures help heal other lives; our very tears help wipe away others' tears."
—Peter Kreeft, *Shared Hells*

REFLECTION

I believed in Jesus's words ... His sincerity, graciousness, and concern for me. God revealed the depth and magnitude of His unconditional love, deeming me worthy, and He rescued me again!

Can you envision Jesus sitting in your presence, wanting to comfort you, wanting to ease your pain, but you refuse Him? Have you ever been so strong-willed or defiant that you thought you didn't need anyone, not even God? If so, what happened to change your mind?

Do you find it hard to let it all go, to give up your struggles, to trust in His love and mercy? Why?

PART TWO

Visions and Dreams

"Call us to hear the voices that challenge …
deep in the hearts of all people.
By serving your world as lovers and dreamers,
we become voices that challenge
for we are the voice of God."

DAVID HAAS, *Voices That Challenge*

Tears from God

Tears rolled down my cheek when God touched me this morning. His presence surrounded me as I stood before Him in church. When I approached the altar, He reached out to embrace me saying, *"I've been waiting for you! I'm so glad you came, and I'm so happy to see you!"*

As He welcomed me, His eyes glistened, and then tears rolled down His cheeks. *"I was hoping you would come today, just to be with Me. I wanted you to feel My presence so I could tell you again I am in your midst! I wanted to remind you to call My name throughout the week! You can talk; I'll listen! You can even be silent in that moment, if that is what you need—if words won't express what you need to say.*

"More importantly, I'll always be waiting to give you My undivided attention. And I want you to tell Me everything that troubles you, everything that lays heavy on your heart or drives you a little crazy, everything that aggravates you or disappoints you, even if you think it is Me. Remember, I am God and I can handle anything.

"I was afraid I wouldn't see you this morning! I've noticed you're overwhelmed and torn, going in too many directions! I know you have so much you feel you need to do or must do, but please, don't compromise yourself! I will provide enough time for what is important!

"I know how busy your life has become, and I'm concerned about you! Seeing the level of stress you function under every day, I want to lighten your load and ease your pain! In a brief moment, think of Me! All you need to do is pause and call out My name! I'm here to protect you and give you peace of mind, to slow the racing pace of your life! I have a plan for your life, and no matter what happens—whether you think it is good or bad, a blessing or tragedy, I will turn everything into My ultimate good!

"Since you came to My House to seek Me today, taking time to fit Me into your schedule, you can rest in My care. You can trust I will bless you

and all that you do for others. I want you to remember and never forget I love you more than you will ever know. I sacrificed My Son for your sins … My arms and tears are for you!"

⌒⌒

"I will instruct you and show you the way you should walk, give you counsel and watch over you."
—Psalms 32:8

"Recognize that God is with you. Acknowledge God knows what He's doing. Search for God's will: the path He desires you to take in life. Consider what God did for you when He sent Jesus to die on the cross."
—Brennan Manning, *The Furious Longing of God*

REFLECTION

I listened as my daughter, a young mother, shared her daily routine. I wept with her as she described how overwhelming her life had become. She was physically tired and mentally challenged by her distress. I recalled how depressed I had become when I had three small children under five, and I could easily relate to her similar circumstance.

A few weeks later, this vision came to me. I saw her entering church one morning, rushing in at the last minute. As she approached the altar, God met her in the aisle and embraced her. "Tears From God" was His conversation with her.

What concerns you the most when you are so busy you wonder how you can do it all? Can you change your daily routine? What can you do right now to ease the stress of your day?

Do you have your priorities in order? Do you need to re-evaluate? If you know your life is complicated, what now … what next?

What are you afraid of? Are you still trying to prove something to yourself or someone else? How do you feel when someone embraces you … blessed, special, loved, or significant?

The Hand of God

Lost somewhere deep within my soul, I desperately prayed and called out to God, longing for some sign or a response, longing for His embrace and hoping to hear Him speak to me. Reaching out, I tried to get His attention, but I felt He was not within my reach. I longed for His presence to comfort me, to give me courage to persevere and not give up. I longed to know I was not alone, and yet, I was alone. I only heard the sound of silence and time stood still.

As my hands continued reaching out to seek God, they longingly clasped together as I prayed for so many things. I offered thanksgiving and praised His Holy Name. I asked for forgiveness and understanding, asking Him to humble me and grant me His wisdom. I asked Him to help me trust in His ways, and I yearned to discover His purpose and plan for my life. I asked Him to teach me the lessons I needed to learn, so I could follow the paths He had chosen for me.

In those moments of silence, I paused in my thoughts until I saw the hand of God reaching out for me. Initially, He didn't grasp hold to comfort me. He gently nudged and reminded me I must move on. He pushed me forward, away from my pain and loneliness. He lit the path of my journey, the one I must make to find myself and return to His love and mercy. He told me what I must still do to find my way back.

Before His arms surrounded me, soothing my heart and comforting my soul, He blessed me with Heavenly peace and told me how much He loved me. My soul's yearning was satisfied; my longing was fulfilled; my loneliness disappeared.

God allowed me to rest in His arms for quite a while before He took my hand. He led me back in time to show me what I had been through, so I could see how far I had already traveled. He exposed my heart and soul to refresh my memory, then He showed me where He has resided within me, helping me understand the depth of His infinite love. He reassured me I was never alone.

Coming back to our present moment together, He revealed, *"I will now call you 'My Chosen One.'"* In His tender and soothing voice, He continued, calmly reminding me, *"In moments of silence, search your heart and call out My name. Seek Me where I reside within you. If you ask for a sign, know in your heart, you will be touched by the hand of God!"*

"God loves us, and yet there is a lurking sense that perhaps you aren't fully part of the us. The arms of God reach to embrace, and somehow you feel yourself just outside God's fingertips."
—Gregory Boyle,
Tattoos on the Heart: The Power of Boundless Compassion

"If we recognize the hand of God, and if we make no opposition in our self-will, we have comfort in our affliction. Happy indeed are those who can bear their sufferings in the enjoyment of this simple peace and perfect surrender to the will of God!"
—Francois Fenlon,
Let Go, Letter 2: "How to Bear Suffering"

"It seems to be a fact that you have to suffer as much from the Church as for it, but if you believe in the divinity of Christ, you have to cherish the world at the same time that you struggle to endure it."
—Flannery O'Connor,
http://spiritualdirection.com/blog/2014/08/13

REFLECTION

I had been living in fear while worrying about my children. When my friend reminded me to trust God, she helped me visualize God's hand of protection guarding them. She encouraged me to entrust all their lives to His care. She helped me release my fear, so I was able to turn my focus back to prayer and place my trust in God's protection.

What do you do when you can't feel God's presence? What do you do when He doesn't answer your immediate need or prayer request? Do you simply wait or do you take things into your own hands? Do you know what you need to do to not lose hope?

Have you ever been disappointed when you were reaching out, knowing you needed someone to help you through a trial, and they were not there for you? Who did you turn to next? What happened? Did you find what you desperately needed? If so, where?

Finally

Thoughts inspired by God were placed in my mind
to lead me down paths with answers to find.
God never lost patience as He guided me;
He never abandoned or failed to protect me.

I had a lifetime to mend and to heal,
and I prayed to believe God's love was real.
My soul was confused, and I hungered for love
and reasons to believe I was worthy of love.

As God promised, He forgave me all of my sins,
but I couldn't forgive myself for the shame I lived in.
Yet amidst my distress, a significant part of my soul
held onto the hope that, one day, I'd be whole.

God silenced Satan's taunting with His Truth and His Word.
He sent disciples and angels to help lead me onward.
One led me on a journey toward His light many days;
she broke through my depression and sad, gloomy haze.

She showed me compassion and guided my thoughts,
and helped me find "myself" and the mind I had lost.
Showered in His wisdom, she helped me survive;
she understood my heartache and pain held inside.

On the paths of my journey, God revealed who I am,
and I finally found comfort by accepting who I am.
He brought others before me who were kind and sincere,
and they helped give me hope and guided me here.

In this here and now, the place that I am,
I am thankful and grateful I am who I am!
Finally!

"God approaches us no matter what the circumstances of our existence. No matter how challenging our situation, God is there, without price, seeking our well-being. In the fullness of God there is room for all souls, room especially for those of us who are seen to be the least desirable and most estranged, those who are cast to the uttermost edges of the world. God's perfection is to welcome the most unloved and unlovely, and to fashion from our imperfect lives a Godlike beauty."

—Craig Rennebohm with David Paul,
Souls in the Hands of a Tender God,
Stories of the Search for Home and Healing on the Streets

REFLECTION

After twenty-two years, I understood what happened, what caused my body to shut down, and it all made sense. I wept uncontrollably in my husband's arms when the answers behind my chronic fatigue (CFS) struck me like a tsunami. Raging, unrelenting waves of tears and years of unresolved searching overcame me. I inhaled relief, exhaled a multitude of unanswered questions that haunted me, because I finally had my answer! Inside the cover of Rennebohm and Paul's book, I wrote:

"Finally! December 2009, my understanding of my Chronic Fatigue Syndrome since July 1987, my long recovery and discovery, my realization after reading *Souls in the Hands of a Tender God*. My journey and healing of my brokenness in body and soul, to finally see it all for what it was and what it is now—fragile, vulnerable, susceptible, sensitive, predisposed, weakened, still seeking answers, seeking to understand, longing for wholeness and peace within my mind and soul! I have finally arrived! I finally understand what happened!"

What have you been seeking? Have you found it yet? Have you been blessed to finally discover what was missing in your life or what caused a significant life-changing event?

Is there something you want or need to figure out in your past? Is there a part of your life you still question? Do you know why it is so important? What do you long to learn or discover?

When God Speaks

When God speaks, He whispers my name to capture my attention. Awakening my soul, He tells me, *"Follow the dreams I've planted in your heart."*

When God speaks, His voice echoes from within me, sparking my yearning to please Him. *"Listen and hear My words of wisdom. I will teach you what is Holy and pure, what is right and just."*

When God speaks, He encourages my effort to walk in His ways and sends His Spirit to comfort me, saying, *"My Spirit will live within your soul. I will guide you and guard you all of My days."*

When God speaks, He urges me to trust Him, advising me to seek answers only from Him. *"Listen closely to My counsel. I will help you understand and learn what is godly and true."*

When God speaks, He convinces me, saying, *"Trust in My ways. I want you to comprehend the significance of My love and concern for you."*

When God speaks, He acknowledges me and lets me know, *"You are on the right path. It is time to begin fulfilling My plan for your life."*

When God speaks, He invites me and inspires me, saying, *"You shall follow in My footsteps to reach your destiny. Allow Me to lead you through the valley of darkness to complete your life journey."*

When God speaks, He nurtures my soul and transforms my heart with His mercy. *"I have forgiven you, now you must forgive those who have trespassed against you, even if you think it is an unforgivable sin. You must forgive yourself once and for all, and let it all go!"*

When God speaks, He teaches me humility and respectfulness toward others. *"Be kind, compassionate, and unconditionally loving. You will touch many lives by serving My poorest of the poor. They will see Me through you, and then believe I am a loving God!"*

When God speaks, He quiets my mind with His heavenly presence. *"Quiet time and prayer with Me will bring you clarity. I will fulfill your need for peaceful awareness, serenity, and inner contentment."*

When God speaks, I listen intently to His promises. *"I will fill your life with hope, increase your confidence and faith, and give you courage to speak out in My Name. I will protect you from evil intentions others try to use to interfere and obstruct your love for Me and My love for you. I will guard your heart and soul from Satan's harm."*

When God speaks, He emphasizes specific things I need to do. *"Be gracious and I will be merciful. Allow Me to replace your weaknesses with fortitude, your fear with self-confidence in Me, your questions with answers, your pride with humility, your pain with healing and comfort. Allow Me to instill unwavering peace in your mind, love in your heart, and hope in your soul. Entrust your entire life with Me!"*

When God speaks, He reminds me what is most important. *"Focus your prayer and attention on our relationship. Your time with Me will be Holy and Sacred. I will satisfy the joy you seek and the love you desperately long to find. Remember My visions. They will appear in your dreams and possibly throughout your day. Be humble and accept them as My will. Follow those dreams, and your life will be complete."*

When God speaks, He expresses His deepest love for me and declares, *"You are My Beloved, and I will always bless you and accept you! In the name of the Father, and the Son, and the Holy Spirit. My peace be with you always! Amen."*

"Suppose someone told you that there was something that spoke to you every night, that always presented you with a truth about your own life, that was tailor-made to your individual needs and particular life story, and that offered to guide you throughout your lifetime and connect you with a source of wisdom far beyond yourself. This is exactly the way it is with our dreams."

—John A. Sanford, *Dreams and Healing:*
A Succinct and Lively Interpretation of Dreams

"There is a deeper voice of God, which you must learn to hear and obey in the second half of life. It will sound an awful lot like the voices of risk, of trust, of surrender, of soul, of 'common sense,' of destiny, of love, of an intimate stranger, of your deepest self, of soulful 'Beatrice.' The true faith journey only begins at this point."

—Richard Rohr, *Falling Upward*

REFLECTION

Has God ever spoken to you? Are you content and comfortable in your relationship with Him? Regardless of how old you are, have you entered or completed a deeper faith journey? If so, what led you to seek answers? Have all of your questions been answered? Do you believe your faith has deepened?

Do you believe God directs your dreams and unconscious moments and thoughts? Do you believe He sends you clear and concise messages and directions for your life? Have you been listening and acting upon them? If not, what holds you back?

Right to Life: A Letter to Dad

Dear and loving Dad,

On the day I was born, Jesus delivered me into His gentle hands. He cradled me, admiring the miracle of life God created in Mom's womb. He breathed on me, and God granted me His gift of Everlasting Life and Eternity in Heaven that very day.

Before taking me Home, Jesus promised, *"You will have the most wonderful life!"* He held me close to His bosom and whispered my name, the one God had chosen for me when I was conceived. He wrapped me in swaddling clothes, just like His mother, Mary, had done for Him.

I closed my eyes to thank God for His abundant love and saving grace, for protecting me from a horrible death. Jesus prayed with Mom, consoling her broken heart, then blessed me with His gifts of incredible joy and peace. Assuring me, He said, *"Your mom will come soon, and your dad will come some time later. One day, you will all be together, but for now, their separation from you is heart-wrenching. This, too, is part of My plan. Our Father and I know and understand their pain!"*

Tenderly, Jesus laid my tiny body in Mary's arms, saying, *"This is My mother! She will love you as much as I love you!"* I looked up and smiled. She was beautiful, kindhearted, and Holy. She beamed with amazing grace when I was in her embrace. Every time she looked at me, I felt her abundant love, as if I were her only son!

Still cradled in her arms, I saw Our Father with tears in His eyes. His gaze was fixed upon me, and He adored me, acknowledging me as His miracle. I smiled at Him, seeing He was so delighted in my presence. *"I allowed you to be conceived, because I knew how much your mom and dad loved each other. You are My gift of life to them, a sign of love for all who believe in Me."*

Dad, even though that was a long time ago, do not feel sad that we have been apart. I have just been waiting to meet up with you. We all knew my life in Mom's womb was short, but Jesus rescued me. He granted me life during birth on the day I was born, the day He brought me into your world.

Like God said, Mom would join me soon in Heaven, and it wasn't long before she came. Since that very day, we have been together, thanking God for your prayers and every tear you have wept out of love for us. We pray for your encouragement and perseverance, sending our smiles upon you when you are overcome with sadness. While waiting for your time to come, we want you to live with joy in your heart. We anticipate the day we will celebrate and be together as God intended!

Every day and night, we pray for your peace of mind, especially when painful memories overwhelm you, especially when you miss us more than your heart can bear. We pray you will be able to allow God's wisdom and strength to release your sadness, because God says, *"Let it go!"*

Every day, we thank God for His miracles of life, and His tender love for all of us. We thank God for your enduring love and belief in Him with all your heart and soul. We see your deep faith and still feel a part of you with us. We thank God for the love you still have for Mom, the love Mom still has for you, and the love you have always had for me! From Heaven above, I love you, too, Dad!

I am, always and forever, your loving son.

"Suppose I return to a scene that causes me much distress … an event that brought me humiliation, like a public rebuke, or one that brought me great pain, like the death of a friend. I relive the whole event, in all its painful detail. I feel once more the pain, the loss, the humiliation, the bitterness. This time, however,

Jesus is there. What role is he playing? Is he a comforter and strengthener? Is he the one who is causing me this pain and loss?"

—Anthony de Mello, an excerpt from *Contact with God:*
Retreat Conferences by Anthony de Mello,
a visualization prayer/meditation

REFLECTION

A fetus is a precious gift of life. In this vision, the unborn child's life was being terminated, but he was saved when God steps in and takes over. Jesus delivered this baby boy, giving him his immediate "Right to Life"!

From Heaven, more than twenty-five years later, this young man tells his dad about his incredible birth and life experience from the moment he was born—when Jesus gave him life in Eternity! I wept as the entire vision unfolded before me during mass. I was amazed God allowed me to observe as Jesus intervened and saved the life of this unborn child, a blessed baby boy!

I pray for all mothers and fathers—may this be a healing message. May God's vision of this birth offer hope, compassion, and understanding for anyone who has experienced a loss … whether it was an abortion, miscarriage, or an attempt to save the mother's life, whether it was an unfortunate illness or accident. May you envision God's hands delivering and saving your child, cradling and breathing life into him or her. Imagine Jesus carrying your child into Everlasting Life. Make room in your mind and heart to hold some part of this vision for the blessing and miracle of life Jesus took to Heaven to wait for you.

Pray until you are able to forgive yourself for what happened that day that changed your life. Let go of your excruciating pain and allow God to bring you a sense of peace—a renewed hope for joining your baby, your child, or your loved one in Heaven. Allow God to ease your grief and heal your heartache, replacing it with His unconditional love, promise of forgiveness, and Divine Mercy.

The Breath of God

God breathes and His breath fills my lungs for the first time,
advancing me from life in the womb to life here on Earth.

God breathes and hopes I accept His Word as Truth and Wisdom,
inspiring me to be a living sign that Christ lives within me.

God breathes and yearns for me to know Him personally,
encouraging me to have a full and loving relationship with Him.

God breathes and instills a longing to follow Him and His ways,
pleasing Him and sharing His gifts, loving and serving the poor.

God breathes and His Spirit fills my soul, increasing my faith,
revealing His plan for me will be fulfilled when I walk with Him.

God breathes and knows I trust and accept Jesus is my Savior,
believing He sent His Son to live, then die on the cross for my sins.

God breathes and offers to replace confusion with peace of mind,
asking me to trust and allow Him to fill my needs and calm my soul.

God breathes and gives me new life when I tell Him I am sorry,
anticipating I will allow His Spirit to restore His love in my heart.

God breathes and assures me to trust in His healing power,
believing unconditional love, forgiveness, and mercy is God given.

God breathes and promises me Eternal Life when I follow Him,
sustaining my life when I intentionally inhale *the breath of God*.

"Prayer is the breath of the soul. Just as breathing is the sign of life, prayer is the sign of the life of the soul."

—Cardinal Henry Edward Manning,
Archbishop of Westminster, *Sins of Omission*

"Breath is giving and receiving, breathing out and in. We can't hold our breath; we cannot clutch the life force. We must surrender to the rhythm and the gift. That is life."

—Richard Fragomeni, *Come to the Feast*

REFLECTION

When you breathe in deeply with intention, filling your lungs to their maximum capacity, imagine the breath of God. Intentionally, take the extended moment to bring God into your thoughts. When you exhale, envision all your turmoil and stress leaving your body and soul.

Have you heard the command "Breathe!"? When you have been overwhelmed, have you ever felt like you wanted to stop breathing? Was someone with you who brought you back to reality … someone who wanted to help you get through whatever your situation was?

Divine Vision

Several years after my best friend died, God granted me this Divine Vision, allowing me to see through the veil and beyond the blindness my grief had caused me. In that moment, He revealed a significant part of me that died along with her. When He reunited her spirit with mine, it was as if He turned back time.

Until now, I couldn't acknowledge the magnitude of my loss. I was unable to admit, let alone accept, how intense my grieving had become, and now, my sadness and deep depression were diminishing my quality of life!

Within this Heavenly vision, I was able to observe until I recognized what I valued in my relationship with her. While in my friend's midst, with God by my side, I was tearfully silent and captivated by her wondrous music. I studied her as she continued playing her piano, harmonizing and pausing from time to time to jot down notes, still rewriting until it sounded just right.

I was fascinated with her renewed godlike nature, unconditional acceptance, and non-judgmental understanding. Her love was immeasurable, her joy was boundless, her music was beautiful! She accepted me as she always had; she joyously loved me like she always did.

She smiled when she noticed us standing there, listening; and then she asked excitedly, *"Do you have your flute with you?"* Smiling, I sighed and paused, shaking my head no. Instantly, I knew that was it … music! She smiled, too, knowing I knew, and with brilliant, sparkling eyes, she revealed, *"Heaven is wonderful! Just you wait! Your time will come soon enough, and I'll be waiting right here for you! We'll play then!"*

And then God smiled! He chuckled intermittently as He lovingly pulled me into His side, knowing His timing was perfect, effective, and powerful! By allowing me to witness this blessed moment while in His embrace, He calmed the immense sadness that had been overtaking my heart. He strengthened my belief by restoring certainty and removing doubt, reaffirming His boundless love and joy for me.

He longed to ease the pain I still felt, to replace the void and emptiness that overwhelmed me with His and her compassion. He saved me from my distress, exchanging it with a renewed internal desire and longing for my Heavenly future! He removed all discouragement from my heart and soul, relieving me of the great burden of grief and sadness that consumed me.

Lingering in His mighty, loving embrace, I was able to comprehend how much I still missed playing my flute with her, being shoulder-to-shoulder sitting on her piano bench, or standing over her right shoulder at the organ. I missed the sensation I had when I leaned into her, connecting as if we were one body and sound of blended music. I remembered being so close, I was consciously aware that we simultaneously breathed in and out together.

We synchronized phrases, reworked harmony, and read from the same sheet music, all while making music together for the glory of God! My longing for that part of Heaven on Earth had been intensifying as I continued to struggle within my soul. I was unconsciously grasping for what was not within my reach or control, no matter how deeply I longed for it or needed it to happen. Oh, how I have missed her presence and the music we made in God's house, but that was not all I was missing!

Our love and concern for each other, our depth of faith, and passion for God and the gifts He gave us was evident in our music during church. And right now, it was everything I was still seeking.

Desperately trying to satisfy the longing in my soul, our relationship and music had become a part of my survival. It kept a sustaining, balanced life force within me, allowing me to feel alive and maintain a connection between God and me, my mind and soul, and living my life being content and having peace of mind. But since she had passed away, what I desperately needed and longed for was God's Heavenly gift and His hope for me—to be healed and whole again, to feel as though I would survive and want to live.

Even though my overwhelming grief and pain were necessary for me, not only to realize what was missing, I needed to understand why. And for me, God revealed wondrous things when I took the time He knew I needed to see more clearly. To see through God's eyes, I found hope, relief, and a new perspective.

While discovering the importance of being able to express myself in the spoken, unspoken, and written word, it is my expression through the gift of music, to be able to play for the glory of God, and to play with her again, that I miss the most!

"But I came to learn that God never shows us something we aren't ready to understand. Instead, He lets us see what we need to see, when we need to see it. He'll wait until our eyes and hearts are open to Him, and then when we're ready, He will plant our feet on the path that's best for us ... but it's up to us to do the walking."

—Immaculee Ilibagiza, *Left to Tell: Discovering God Amidst the Rwandan Holocaust*

"It is important for our personal growth, both spiritual and emotional, that we resolve these unresolved situations that keep rankling within us. When we relive them in the company of Christ, again and again, if need be, we will notice that a new meaning comes into them, that the sting goes out of them, that we can now return to them without any emotional upset; in fact, that we can even return to them now with a sense of gratitude to God, who planned these events for some purpose that will rebound to our benefit and to His glory. This form of prayer is good therapy and good spirituality."

—Anthony de Mello, an Excerpt from *Contact with God: Retreat Conferences by Anthony de Mello*

REFLECTION

God granted me "Divine Vision" because He knew I was ready. He knew I needed to know what I couldn't seem to figure out on my own. He knew I would finally understand.

If you are still longing for understanding, are you seeking it spiritually? Do you have faith it will come?

Has God given you a vision and/or a gift of understanding you truly needed? If so, have you been able to move on in your life after He revealed His wisdom to you? Have you found a renewed sense of peace?

PART THREE

Prayers

"When I feel all sick inside
with no safe place to hide,
God I need you to listen.
When it seems I can't go on
then I long to hear the song
reminding me you are my friend."

DAVID HAAS, *With You By My Side*

My Prayers for You

I trust and believe my prayers for you are being answered. I pray yours are being answered, too!

May you find encouragement and hope, especially when you feel you desperately need it and your spirits need lifting.

May you always have someone you can turn to when you need a friend, especially when you are lost or feel lonely, abandoned or afraid.

May you learn what you need to know and find the answers you seek, especially when you have a longing to figure out your life.

May you be blessed with God's understanding and clarity. Be grateful if you already know your purpose in life.

May you discover and trust what is God's will for your life, then follow your passion to make a difference in this world.

May you seek God when you realize something is missing in your life, especially when what you are missing is time with Him.

May you find words to express yourself and speak in a calm and loving voice to everyone, especially family and your children.

May you always be kind and find appropriate words to express yourself when others' actions or your life is disappointing.

May you speak openly about your anger. Unresolved anger turned inward becomes depression. Talk to God, talk it out, and work it out.

May you find time for God and seek His guidance and wisdom, knowing a relationship with Him can bring you peace and contentment.

May you make time for your family and children a priority. It is a great investment. Life goes on and children grow up. Don't be sorry.

May you admit your error when you are mistaken and be considerate when it is the other way around. Remember, tables do turn.

May you find love and joy, laughter and happiness. Your joy will be multiplied by sharing your time and blessings with others.

May you be supportive of others' accomplishments. Be satisfied with what you have and where you are in life—or make a change!

May your relationships at home be filled with unending love, sharing responsibilities and finances. In marriage, two become *one*!

May you treat all others with respect, even when it is difficult, especially when they have hurt you, especially when it is family.

May you be blessed with the ability to be sincere and trustworthy toward all people, especially those you love.

May you take care of yourself. Eat well in moderation. Sleep when you are supposed to. Get exercise and fresh air every day.

May you stop beating yourself up. We all make mistakes. We all have sinned. Seek forgiveness for yourself.

May you never lose hope! If you read His Word, you will find all your answers and your faith will be increased!

May you trust your life with God, because everything is in His hands. Even with free will, God will see you are going to be okay!

May your presence, footsteps, and journey lead you to make a positive and loving difference in the lives of other people.

May you believe you will not be forgotten, because someone will always be waiting for you in this life and life ever after.

May you be the blessing others seek. Be the person they need to give them hope! Make them feel loved, accepted, and worthy.

May others see you are walking in His footsteps. Ask them to follow Him with you. They may be just waiting for you to ask them.

May you learn life lessons that will enrich your soul when you become an example of loving service to those in need. You will learn from one another when you help each other.

May you be willing to trust enough to turn and go in a different direction, especially when God has provided a new path for you.

May you be strong enough to surrender your inner struggles, then follow where God leads you. Let go and let God.

May you recognize Christ lives among us. Be compassionate and humble. Do what you can for someone in need.

May you believe everything God has told you is true. Have an open mind to experience and accept the lessons you need to learn.

May you find courage to begin again if your journey disappoints you. Turn to God for direction, turn back, or take a new road.

May you seek forgiveness when feel you have failed God, your family, or friends. Ask for God's mercy when you say, "I am sorry."

May you trust in God's mighty power whenever you struggle. He will shield you, protect you, and provide what you need to survive.

May the warmth of His Holy Spirit soothe your soul, and may His light shine to encourage you and encourage others.

May you forgive others, whether they say they are sorry or not. Grant them forgiveness. Withholding forgiveness punishes you.

May you know and believe, with all your heart and soul, our God is a loving God, and He deems you worthy of great things.

May you always know you are loved and realize you have so much to be thankful for!

"In prayer I always find light and strength of spirit although there are moments so trying and hurtful, that it is sometimes difficult to imagine that these things can happen in a convent. Strangely, God sometimes allows them, but always in order to manifest or develop virtue in a soul. That is the reason for trials."
—Saint Faustina Kowalska, *The Diary of Saint Faustina*

REFLECTION

Has someone prayed with you, and they seemed to know your heart and pain, what you needed, and how to ask God? Were their prayers another reassuring sign of God's hope for your life? Did you feel God's presence while you were together? What is your prayer for yourself today?

Do you feel Christ's presence and outpouring of love when you help or pray for others? What is your prayer for someone else today?

God's Prayer

My outstretched arms are for you, a sign of how much I love you. Whether you realize it or not, I am in your presence. I assure you, I surround you with boundless unconditional love and understanding.

I long for you to want to spend time with Me. I long to have a relationship with you, because I created you to be My companion. I pray for you to open your heart to love Me, to trust and believe in Me. I hope you will discover contentment and peace of mind when we are together, that it will spill over into your everyday life. I want to ease your pain and heal your brokenness, and I long to restore a positive and hopeful sense of well-being within you!

When Jesus was scourged and nailed to His cross, until He died a terrible death, I felt every moment of His agony. I watched the brutality, injustice, and pain people intentionally caused Him! I sacrificed My Son for you, yet I watch your trials and the crosses you bear every day … you were worth My sacrifice. The magnitude of pain Jesus endured was a sign of Our infinite love for you.

I urge you to stop fighting your battles alone, because I have already fought and won them for you! If only you would let them go, I could release the grasp they have on your life. At this point, what do you have to lose? I will replace your struggles with My love. I will fulfill My promises of hope and healing. I will restore your life, because I am your mighty and powerful God!

I will wait patiently for your surrender. If only you would give Me your heartache and disappointments, I could remove the weight and distress these burdens have caused you. I assure you, you will regain your perspective when I lift your load, when you allow Me to do this for you.

Place your trust in Me. I will help you endure and survive this world, but I want so much more for you—I want you to thrive! I want you to be happy and enjoy your life! I want you to learn your lessons, find your way, and seek the path I have prepared for you. I promise to bless you amidst it all, because there is so much more I want to share with you. Open your heart and allow Me to show you the way to Everlasting Life is through Me.

Granting you eternal hope, God.

⌒

"Recognize that God is with you. Acknowledge God knows what He's doing. Search for God's will: the path He desires you to take in life. Consider what God did for you when He sent Jesus to die on the cross."

—Brennan Manning, *The Furious Longing of God*

"By rising from the dead—the Lord rescued all that is good, holy and true about what it means to be free, to thrive, to fully be who we really are. For each of us personally, this means, if we humbly ask Him, He not only removes the barriers of sin that imprison us in all kinds of falsehoods. He also reveals the truth about who He created us to be, and in revealing this truth, He establishes us in it. To finally be free, to finally be who we truly are—this is what the Lord wants for us."

—Anthony Lillies, *The Life of Prayer: The Sure Path to Freedom*
October 11, 2014. http://spiritualdirection.com

REFLECTION

In Mel Gibson's movie *The Passion*, explicit scenes portrayed what Jesus endured from Gethsemane until His death on the cross. Watching the movie, I witnessed the magnitude of barbaric torture and horrendous cruelty during His scourging. I saw Mary's unimaginable agony as she heard people ridicule, taunt, and scoff at her Son. Jesus struggled to carry His own cross, until a man stepped forward to carry it for Him. I witnessed Mary's incredible faith and intense, unspeakable grief and anguish. I saw there was nothing she could do but trust in her Lord, knowing Jesus was going to be crucified. While on the cross, Jesus said, *"Father, forgive them for they know not what they have done."* And I wept.

Have you held onto things that have happened, including painful relationships, repeating in your mind what someone said or did to intentionally hurt you? Does it keep haunting and taunting you? What holds you back from letting go of the pain, from forgiving those who have deeply wounded you? Have you asked God to help you let go? Do you question God's ability to take your pain away?

My Journey and Prayer

My God, accept me as I am and forgive me for venturing off Your path of righteousness. Please light Your path, so I may find my way back. Help me see how I have erred, so I may learn from my mistakes and change my ways. Guide me forward when You decide I am ready, and lead me where you want me to go next.

My God, help me discern when I am heading in the wrong direction. When I lose sight of what is important, help me know what is right and just. When my workload and worldly desires begin to interfere with Your will for my life, give me perspective and help me see through Your eyes. Every time I have lost my way, I long for You to rescue me so I can follow You!

My God, bless me with empathy and compassion for others who struggle and feel their life is difficult. Help me show them they will not only survive their journey, they can thrive and continue on!

My God, please grant me courage and self-confidence to give witness so others will be able to see You live within me, so they will know You have saved my life! I hope they will be able to see, hear, and trust in You as I have learned to trust in You. May they become a witness, too, realizing You are a loving and compassionate God. You are the great I AM.

My God, I ask for Your wisdom to guide me. Please grant me fortitude to persevere and strength to endure because I need You for whatever lies ahead! Open my eyes to see and my mind to know, my heart to feel and my soul to believe Your love is unconditional, Your Word is Divine Truth, and Your glorious promise of Everlasting Life is for me.

My God, thank you for loving me as I am, helping me grow deeper in faith, and leading me on this journey. Your presence has given me hope, Your protection has saved me, and Your mercy has restored my soul.

My God, thank you for traveling with me. I am grateful You have been nudging me, carrying me, embracing me, and praying for me. Thank you for every blessing and struggle; each joy and sorrow; times of sickness, darkness, and health; as well as what you have withheld from my life to humble me. I am "who I am" because You love me!

My God, whatever my future holds for me, wherever my journey leads, when my time comes, may I be ready when You beckon me, *"Come Home!"*

"Suffering, failure, loneliness, sorrow, discouragement, and death will be part of your journey, but the Kingdom of God will conquer all these horrors. No evil can resist grace forever."
—Brennan Manning, *The Ragamuffin Gospel: Good News for the Bedraggled, Beat-Up, and Burnt Out*

"You're no longer fighting God, trying to make Him do what you want. You're accepting what happens, and your main prayer transforms into one that asks God for nothing more than understanding and perhaps strength to endure."
—Amy Welborn, *Prove It!*

REFLECTION

As you ponder your life, do you feel God has enlightened you? Do you feel compelled to share that wisdom with someone? If so, who?

What were your significant lessons—those you have learned over your lifetime that were directly related to your faith or belief in God?

Do you feel as though you have gained a renewed spiritual strength, knowing you can endure whatever comes along?

Come, Holy Spirit! Come!

Come, Holy Spirit! Come! Be present in the flame that lights our way and warms our hearts with compassion, illuminating our vision of God's love. Be found in our loving kindness, like a mother caring for her newborn child, as we comfort those in need—within our families, our communities, and throughout the world.

Come, Holy Spirit! Come! Be present in the voice we hear and the words we speak, sharing God's Truth with others. Whenever someone is seeking guidance and direction, lead them according to Your will and help restore peace and joy in their heart so they may share it with others, too.

Come, Holy Spirit! Come! Be present in the prayers we offer, the music of our souls, and the songs we sing. Be present in our actions as we share gifts God has given us with others less fortunate. Be a visible sign and our inspiration for unconditional loving support to help all people!

Come, Holy Spirit! Come! Be present in the promise that fills our hearts with hope when we are struggling so we can pass the same hope onto others. Help us recognize everyday blessings and miracles, especially when we care for one another as God intends us to do.

Come, Holy Spirit! Come! Be present in every embrace and each time we greet one another. Be witnessed in the smile on our faces, the twinkle and tears in our eyes, and our day-to-day actions. Encourage us to rejoice with gladness and sing Your praises always, but especially when others are discouraged. Guide us to be their light of hope.

Come, Holy Spirit! Come! Be present in our anticipation as we wait each year for Jesus's birth. May the Star of Bethlehem remind us and lead us to find a babe lying in a manger. As prophecies foretold, God fulfilled His promise—His only Son, the Messiah, would be born in the City of David. Remind us how great His love is and be with us as we remember He came to die for our sins.

Come, Holy Spirit! Come! Be present in our inspiration when we come together as God's chosen people, especially when we gather to pray and help others. Guide us as we witness and give testimony of our faith.

Come, Holy Spirit! Come! Be our sign of hope and love that encourages us to be Christ-like in our everyday lives. Teach us how to live as Jesus commanded us to do: *"Love your neighbor as yourself."* Lead us to follow in His footsteps and be present with Him in each moment, like Mary, Martha's sister, at the feet of Jesus when He came to their home.

Come, Holy Spirit! Come! Be the living sign that Christ's presence lives within us. May each one of us be an example of God's love through our acts of kindness and generosity, our sincere and caring manner by showing God's mercy is for all people!

Come, Holy Spirit! Come!

"When the time for Pentecost was fulfilled, they were all in one place together. And suddenly there came from the sky a noise like a strong driving wind, and it filled the entire house in which they were. Then there appeared to them tongues as of fire, which parted and came to rest on each one of them. And they were all filled with the Holy Spirit and began to speak in different tongues, as the Spirit enabled them to proclaim."

—Acts 2:1–4

"Please pass me the Cup, Lord. It's as necessary for me as it was for You. Give me strength and courage, because what I ask is a fearful thing to me. Change me into a vessel fit for receiving, not only what You would have for me, but also whom You would have me become. I have no strength to do this but by You. Strip me of me, and replace it with You. Have Your own way with me. Thy will be done on earth—my earth, my life—as it is in Heaven. Amen."

—Greg Harris, *The Cup and the Glory,*
Lessons on Suffering and the Glory of God

REFLECTION

As time passes, ask God for what you need, and then trust and wait for His response. Allow Him to decide if it is in accord with His will, because He may have a better plan. Learn to accept what He blesses you with and be patient in His timing, regardless of what is going on in your life.

Do you feel or have you felt the presence of the Holy Spirit? Have you reached out and touched someone else's life? Do you believe the Holy Spirit was moving you or prompting you to take action?

What do you experience when you help and serve others? What do others seem to appreciate most? Is it your time, your kindness, simply showing them you care, etc.?

What are a few of your most recent blessings? Have you discovered unexpected blessings, even when things did not turn out as you originally hoped or prayed for?

My God

~~~~~~~~~~~~~~~~~~~~

Infinite, loving Creator—my God. I have lost touch with my soul. I don't even know who I am anymore.

My God, please accept me as I am—lonely, broken, and unworthy. I long for Your embrace to give me hope and protect me from this world; at times, even from myself. Please seek me in the lost realm of my forsaken dungeon of depression. Please reach out for me, and guide my way back to You. Be the light that shines in the dark, and restore my sight so I may recognize You and see Your presence again in my life.

My God, please bring awareness and a keen intuition of Satan within my consciousness. Please fight for me when I can no longer fight on my own. Help me remain steadfast whenever evil attempts to destroy me. Help me endure his torture before he restricts my ability to persevere against him, before he has silenced me so I can no longer call out for You.

My God, please remove Satan's authority over me. Sever the bondage he uses to strangle my spirit and choke all desire for life out of me. Guard my soul when Satan begins to diminish, punish, or break me down with his emotional abuse.

My God, help me forgive myself for the sins of my heart, mind, and soul. Help me let go of each memory of my past that was not seeking you or honorable in Your eyes. Please show me how to forgive those who have sinned against me, especially those who were led by Satan himself. Help me see their ulterior motives; deception; and intentional, devious manipulation. Open my eyes so I may see through the shame he uses to overshadow and blind me. Help me discern and recognize Satan and his followers before I am feeling worthless and undeserving, yet another time.

My God, please redeem my soul, and reclaim me as Your follower! I long to return to You, to renew my relationship and pledge a new vow with You. I know You are a loving and forgiving God—You are my God! Humble me in Your presence with Your tender mercy. Please mend my heart and soul; please heal my spiritual brokenness and ongoing fatigue. Grant me wisdom and help me attain emotional and mental stability. I want to grow beyond what keeps holding me back.

My God, please help me rebuild who I am meant to be in Your image. Reveal what You see in my reflection so I may see what You believe in me, so I may recognize the woman You created me to be. Please help me refocus my mind and soul only on You. Show me ways to earn Your respect, so I may bring You honor once again and believe I am worthy of Your love.

My God, please grant me Your saving grace, especially when I am losing another battle in my mind and soul. Whenever I am devastated and feel hopeless, when I have completely lost all my strength once again, I begin to wonder if I will survive. Please intervene and restore my sanity; transform my fear into confidence and trust in You! Please continue to help me surrender; purify and cleanse my soul so I may do Your will. Lead me and I will follow; carry me when I am too weak and unable to see.

My God, show me how to serve Your people in ways that are pleasing only to You. Open my ears to hear Your voice and remind me to listen to Your words of Truth. Encourage me when I need Your strength to sustain me. Help me see and know Your will and desire for me in this world.

My God, I am Yours forevermore. Please save me, I pray!

"Therefore, that I might not be too elated, a thorn in the flesh was given to me, an angel of Satan, to beat me, to keep me from being too elated. Three times I begged the Lord about this—that it might leave me, but he said to me, *"My grace is sufficient for you, for my power is made perfect in weakness."* I will rather boast most gladly of my weaknesses, in order that the power of Christ may dwell with me. Therefore, I am content with weaknesses, insults, hardships, persecutions, and constraints, for the sake of Christ; for when I am weak, then I am strong."

—II Corinthians 12:7–10

REFLECTION

It was November 1993 when I began my spiritual journey. I finally realized how depressed I was when I attended a retreat. The morning speaker shared stories similar to mine and posed many questions I needed to answer for myself. I needed help to find my way, and my journey was just beginning.

During this presentation, I witnessed a voice of experience—a loving spirit exuding compassion, empathy, and strength for having survived clinical depression and devastating life challenges. I was given hope that day, realizing I was desperately longing for God's joy to return in my heart, allowing me to recover, but also believing I could recover!

It wasn't long before I was in weekly counseling sessions, discovering where my life went off track. I had to learn how to put my despair into words before I could speak and write about how I truly felt. I had to discover what caused me to become so lost.

My counselor and I prayed together, asking for God's guidance and protection on my journey. I began to understand and accept myself in the present state my mind was in, all while desperately seeking the person I wanted to become. While searching and reliving painful events, I was able to discover my way back to stability and wellness once again.

Under God's direction, I was easily convinced there was hope for me! Since I was extremely weak and compromised, desperately longing for answers, I needed someone to lead me back to a life of hope and joy. My counselor helped guard my soul and stood in the gap with God many times to shield me from Satan, denying any of his power to harm me or mark my soul. Satan became fierce, like a wolf waiting to attack and devour me whenever he sensed I was vulnerable and lost. Whenever I was slipping into darkness or fear of abandonment, Satan was unrelenting and continued to haunt me.

Once I began to make progress, I was able to go forward with my life. With gentle guidance and direction, I was discovering my own answers, knowing God's unconditional love and mercy was meant for me! Counseling sessions helped me in so many ways by giving me encouragement, inspiration, and hope.

As time passed, God soothed my pain and healed my brokenness. I eventually discovered the joy and peace I sought couldn't be found outside of who I was—it was found within me through my relationship with God!

Has someone made a profound difference in your life? Did you learn certain things from him or her that changed your outlook on life or helped bring you out of the darkness you were lost in?

If you've been seeking peace and joy, have you found it? Did you discover it on your own or through someone who helped guide you?

If you haven't found your joy, what do you need to do? Who would you turn to who can help you find it?

Have you ever walked with someone else on their journey? Did you know what they were seeking? Did they find it?

A Child of God

Dear Lord, I pray …
Forgive me for the faults I see and those I do not see.
Help me envision peacefulness; help me see I am free.
Please humble me and calm the raging force inside my soul.
May I accept Your grace and love; may I believe I am whole.

I pray for your protection, as I ponder what I will do.
I pray I will know within my heart Your love will carry through.
Lord of Lords, Our Father, help me clearly hear Your voice.
May I receive Your wisdom to guide my thoughts, my choice.

I pray for Your eternal love, that I may also be
a sign of Your unending love … a child of God … me!

"But to those who did accept him, he gave power to become children of God, to those who believe in his name."
—John 1:12

"But if any of you lacks wisdom, he should ask of God who gives to all generously and ungrudgingly, and he will be given it."
—James 1:5

REFLECTION

As I began to pray more and more, it became quite clear what I longed for—I wanted to be *a child of God* and loved unconditionally. I wanted to become someone He would be proud of.

How do you envision God? How would you describe Him to someone who has never heard of Him? How would you explain your relationship with your Heavenly Father?

What was your relationship like with your own father? Were you close? Was he always there for you? If not, do you know why?

Be with Me, I Pray

Lord, be with me, I pray. In this moment, breathe the power of Your life into my soul. Surround me with Your presence and unconditional love. Protect me from Satan's harmful ploys because he is delighting in my pain. He thinks he has succeeded in breaking me down, burying me alive within my mind and soul, destroying me once and for all. Paralyzed and suffocating, show me my life is worth saving, because I need a sign!

Purify my heart and mind. Bring clarity and visions of Your hand protecting me. Keep me safe in Your care and give me strength to endure and survive, to be strong enough to stand on my own before You. Listen as I speak of my burdens and disappointments that diminish my life. Help me be open and share everything that leaves me feeling helpless and hopeless. My Lord, please have mercy on my soul.

When I am lost, I feel unworthy. Light Your path so I will not wander aimlessly in darkness. Reach out for me and lead me toward Your guiding light. Show me what You still see in me, because I can't see my reflection anymore. I have lost sight of all goodness within me—I see nothing of interest or value in my soul.

My God, seek me because I am so weak I can no longer seek You. Search for me in the depths of despair that smother me because my desire to fight for life is quickly disappearing.

O Lord, grant me Your wisdom because I can't discern what is truthful and what is not. Forgive my past and present states of mind when I continue to lose my sense of self. Take hold of my life and direct me in righteous ways. Humble me and forgive me for those times I searched for love in the wrong places, those times I had no right to justify my actions. Lift my soul with Your mighty power and release the chains Satan uses to imprison me.

Lord, please answer my plea when I see how desperately I need You, because I know I cannot make it on my own. As I surrender to Your will, free me from the bondage of disillusionment that prevents me from knowing and trusting You are here. Show me how to give my life to You. Enlighten me with Your words of encouragement when I fail.

Lord, keep pursuing me, because I keep losing myself! Accept me every time I seek You and hold me in Your embrace. Please grant me a vision of hope for Everlasting Life with You! Lord, be with me, I pray!

"When we find ourselves in a midlife depression, suddenly hate our spouse, our jobs, our lives—we can be sure that the unlived life is seeking our attention. When we feel restless, bored, or empty, despite an outer life filled with riches, the unlived life is asking us to engage. To not do this work will leave us depleted and despondent, with a nagging sense of ennui or failure. As you may have already discovered, doing or acquiring more does not quell your unease or dissatisfaction. Neither will 'meditating on the light' or attempting to rise above the sufferings of earthly existence. Only awareness of your shadow qualities can help you to find an appropriate place for your unredeemed darkness and thereby create a more satisfying experience. To not do this work is to remain trapped in the loneliness, anxiety, and dualistic limits of the ego instead of awakening to your higher calling."
—Robert A. Johnson, *Owning Our Own Shadow*

"Have no anxiety at all, but in everything, by prayer and petition, with thanksgiving, make your requests known to God. Then the peace of God that surpasses all understanding will guard your hearts and minds in Christ Jesus."

—Philippians 4:6–7

"No matter how much light I carry within me, there will always be times of feeling lost, being confused, seeking direction. It is the way of the human heart."

—Joyce Rupp, *The Star in My Heart:*
Experiencing Sophia, Inner Wisdom

REFLECTION

I know I have great faith, but something still triggers me to lose myself somewhere within my mind. I know I am susceptible to additional "crashes" and episodes because they keep reoccurring. I live on the edge each time my mind becomes unstable, since I have discovered each subsequent incident is more significant and frightening than the last. I have learned to accept my limitations, and when I realize I am becoming entrapped again, I always seek professional counseling, my doctor's guidance, and reconsider medication options. Since I barely survived the last severe episode of depression, I know I must seek help sooner. Realizing I have never been able to recover on my own, I know what I must do when depression begins to invade me. I must not deny or delay my need for intervention and loving care. Even though I understand more about my mind and body connection, I am still vulnerable.

On my journey of life, I live moment by moment. I consciously live in the presence of caring people; they help sustain a balance in my life. I acknowledge my need for acceptance, loving relationships, and God's continual presence in my thoughts and prayers. He guides and protects me, guards my heart and soul, and blesses me with His embrace and unconditional love.

Have you encountered Satan at some point in your life? Were you able to recognize when you were in the presence of evil?

Has Satan ever led you away from God? What did he tempt you with? What did you have to lose if you kept going in his direction?

Did God intervene when you were amidst a great battle? Did God reveal Himself to you, so you would know He was there to protect you, to fight for your soul, and help you endure? Did He send someone else or a warrior to help defeat Satan?

If you have successfully denied Satan or escaped Satan's hold on your life, was that the end of it? Did Satan return again and continue to cause you harm and discontent while still trying to break you?

Has Satan ever turned his fury upon you, causing you to fear him and what he threatened to do to you? If Satan succeeded or tried to make you feel unworthy of a better life, ashamed of yourself, or worthless, what did he say or do to you? Does he still threaten you?

PART FOUR

Blessings

"Rejoice and be glad!
Blessed are you, holy are you!
Rejoice and be glad!
Yours is the kingdom of God!"

DAVID HAAS, *Blest Are They*

My Angel's Mission

God chose for me an angel, the one He knew I'd need,
to help me find my way, to come and rescue me!
God admired my angel's progress, since she was here before,
then trained her how to listen and to guide so I'd learn more.

He told her what to do and say to touch my heart and soul,
"Give her insight to her past; share what's made you whole."
She started out by saying, *"God knows I'll understand.
I have struggled and survived—my life is in His hands!"*

This was how it all began, the first time our souls met,
she shared things that God had said, *"You are Heaven sent!
He granted me His wisdom to give you hope this day,
to walk along beside you and help you see His way!*

*"He said He watched you go astray, down paths of self-destruct,
discouraged by your actions, being confused by whom to trust.
He talked about your darkness, the shame within your soul,
while seeking love you could not find and longing to be whole.*

*"Since you are lost inside your mind, I was sent to lead you back.
I'm here to say He loves you and will always take you back!"*
She taught me how to grieve and cry and let go of my pain.
She showed me how to love myself and smile amidst the rain.

She helped me through my loneliness and times of great despair.
She insisted, *"You are not alone; His arms are always near!"*
I learned from her compassion, her dear and loving soul—
she convinced me, *"You are worthy; God's love will make you whole.*

"So take a breath and calm your soul, take as many as you need.
Breathe in and out, and let it go; turn away from sin to see!
Envision a place that's peaceful, to hold within your mind—
a place that brings contentment, while there, He'll ease your mind!

"Also, find an image of the person you'd like to be,
and send your prayers to Heaven, only He can set you free!"
My angel taught me about myself while searching through my past.
I discovered "who I am" through Him; then forgave myself, at last!

She helped me make some changes by simplifying my life to see
I was blessed more than I knew, and God had set me free!
Now I believe, with all my heart, in angels from above,
and I believe, with all my soul, she was sent to me with love!

∽

"For I am the LORD, your God, who grasps your right hand; it is
I who say to you, 'Fear not, I will help you!'"
—Isaiah 41:13

"Be a presence of hope wherever you go. The interior journey is nigh possible to make without gathering strength and inspiration from those who have made the passage before us."
—Joyce Rupp, *Open the Door, A Journey to the True Self*

"If we all carry a little of the burden, it will be lightened. If we share in the suffering of the world, then some will not have to endure so heavy an affliction. You may think you are alone, but we are all members of one another. We are children of God together."
—Dorothy Day, *Catholic Worker Movement*

REFLECTION

Shirley Wuerth and my counselor were angels on a mission. When I attended my first Grief Recovery workshop with Shirley, we had our own losses, but we also shared many similar trials and personal struggles. Shirley had already survived what I was going through, and we needed each other more than ever!

Do you have an angel, someone who carried a specific message from God to you? Have you ever felt that you were God's messenger, that you were chosen to share His message with someone going through a similar struggle? If so, have you felt the blessing was two-fold—as much for them as it was for you?

A Woman of God

Awoman of God lives in unity with His Spirit! The depth of her love and relationship with the Holy Trinity is evident in how she lives every day. She holds onto His promise of everlasting love and Everlasting Life, and she walks on paths journeying to her inmost soul. Along the way, she finds God anticipating her arrival, looking forward to her music for all of Heaven and Earth.

As far back as she can remember, He has found her worthy. He still blesses her with an incredible gift of music. She is humbled by His faith and trust in her, and she always prays to invoke His Holy Spirit for guidance. She leads His chosen people in chant and song, and He delights in her sincere, unswerving willingness to share her gift with others. He inspires her, and she honors Him by singing and arranging music that is pleasing to Him. In turn, her music inspires His people! Harmony flows from within her, and a heavenly peace surrounds everyone in her presence. Her passion, contentment, and expression of love for God is reflected in her music and her soul!

Blessed are they who have crossed her path and heard her play …
those who found her music inspiring!

Blessed are they who have made music with her …
those who sang, played, and harmonized together!

Blessed are they who have met at God's house …
those who gathered to worship and praise His Holy Name!

Blessed are they who have been considered her family and friends …
those who prayed and shared God's gift of Spirit with her!

Blessed are they who have missed her body and soul,
her heart and music …
those who are reminded of her love and still hear her music!

For everyone who knew her, these were her prayers for all of you:

"May the song of your soul never fall silent. May God's Spirit also find a dwelling place within you. May your relationship with Him fulfill your longing and yearning heart. May His presence help you understand the meaning of your life. May you be blessed with His gift of music for you to share with others. May God's peace always be with you!"

"Justice and judgment are the foundation of your throne; love and loyalty march before you. Happy the people who know you, LORD, who walk in the radiance of your face. In your name they sing joyfully all the day."
—Psalm 89:15–17

"Do not say, I follow the one true path of the Spirit, but rather, I have found the Spirit walking on my path, for the Spirit walks on all paths."
—Khalil Gibran, *The Prophet*

REFLECTION

Shirley Wuerth was a woman of God, and she blessed my life in so many ways. She understood and shared the depth of music in her soul—the gifts God gave her. She helped teach me how to love, forgive, and move on. She shared her heart and soul with me, as I did with her, and she helped me understand the importance of loving relationships and being spiritually connected with others. Since she passed away, I still long for her and pray that I may also be *a woman of God*.

If you have a close, spirit-filled relationship with someone, do you feel closer to God while in his or her presence?

Can you rightfully say, "I am a woman, man, or child of God"?

Music

~~~~~~~~~~~~~~~~

Music repeats itself over and over in my mind. Even in holy silence, I hear a faint melody; I feel a subtle rhythm in my soul. Music beckons me to listen closely, to keep an even tempo. Occasionally, I feel free to interpret how it has moved me, and sometimes, I am inspired to write.

Psalms, written by simple men who feared the Lord, still send messages to all God's people. Even though thousands of years have passed, the words and love songs still enrich me. Their rhythmic pace and ritualistic patterns speak to me, and a calming sense of ancient wisdom enters my existence. I feel as though God is actually connecting my soul with old biblical times.

In the presence of music, I am often keenly aware God is within me. He soothes my heart and soul when He fills the voids of my life with perfect harmony and rhythm. He encircles me with His protection. All my earthly concerns seem so insignificant when He inspires me, granting music to evolve and move my heart and soul. Even though my ability to hear may fade from time to time, He never hesitates to whisper to me or chant once more. When He redirects my attention back to Him, He restores my soul once again!

Always desiring an intimate relationship with my Savior, I continually seek my Lord and my God, praying for a Heavenly sense of reassurance to envelop me. I hear Him remind me, *"I will grant fulfillment of your heart's desires if they are according to My will. Amidst your earthly trials, I am pleased to see your deep faith and trust in Me. I will answer prayers asked in My name. You may or may not like My answer, but I have your best interest at heart!"*

I smile in acknowledgment, accept His blessings, and bow in reverence. I am humbled, eternally grateful, and my heart is full.

Thanks be to God! Amen!

"17th March 1870 ... O Plato! O Pythagoras! Ages ago you heard these harmonies, surprised these moments of inward ecstasy, knew these divine transports! If music thus carries us to heaven, it is because music is harmony, harmony is perfection, perfection is our dream, and our dream is heaven. This world of quarrels and of bitterness, of selfishness, ugliness, and misery, makes us long involuntarily for the eternal peace, for the adoration, which has no limits, and the love, which has no end. It is not so much the infinite as the beautiful that we yearn for. It is not being, or the limits of being, which weigh upon us; it is evil, in us and without us. It is not at all necessary to be great, so long as we are in harmony with the order of the universe. Moral ambition has no pride; it only desires to fill its place, and make its note duly heard in the universal concert of the God of love."

—Henri-Frédéric Amiel, *Amiel's Journal:*
The Journal Intime of Henri-Frédéric Amiel

"Music expresses that which cannot be said and on which it is impossible to be silent."

—Victor Hugo, *Les Misérables*

REFLECTION

Does music inspire and/or move you? When you listen to music, do you hear more than just the words? Do the sounds surround you or evolve from within you? If music has ever brought you to tears, do you know why?

How does music fit into your life? Is music a significant part of who you are?

During church services, do you sing along with the choir and congregation? If not, why?

The Fabric of Me

Out of respect for myself, I must say
I have so much to learn to grow each new day.
God and relationships are important in my life—
family and friends and being a wife.

God fashioned my pattern with boundaries for me.
He said, *"Pay attention. Never lose sight of Me!"*
In dark shadows, I lost Him and my sense of self,
but the weave in my pattern is the fabric of self.

Past lessons, like threads, appeared clear and defined—
some simple, some not, but all of them mine.
Textured threads of deep color
created scenes beautiful, bright, and pure.
Intermingled with unraveled, some dull and dark, some impure.

Impure were temptations, impure thoughts and being lured;
I was living in confusion, being tested, and unsure.
Threads dark and misshapen, twisted and deformed
were lessons so painful or caused someone harm.

Threads of no color were the times I was lost;
I had no sense of being, though inside I fought.
Sometimes my fabric was drab, smooth, and so plain,
but now its dimensions and depths have all changed.

A new weave in my fabric has now taken form—
there is only one like it; by God's hand, it transformed.
Where it is colorful and bright, it shows times I survived,
I was blessed, I was saved, and my soul came alive!

I follow His pattern and He guides me to see
only we are the weavers of the fabric of me.
"You'll know when it's complete; by its beauty, you'll see!"
Then, He told me He is proud of *the fabric of me*!

"Begin to weave and God will give you the thread."
—*German Proverb*

"An invisible red thread connects those who are destined to meet, regardless of time, place, or circumstance. The thread may stretch or tangle, but will never break."
—*Ancient Chinese Proverb*

"Life has many twists and turns, and each of us has a destiny to follow and fulfill that is like a thread that weaves its way in and out of all that happens to us. Our dreams help us find and follow this thread. We need this help, for otherwise the way is easily lost. When we lose the thread, the dreams tell us that we have gone off the path. When we have found the thread, the dreams tell us which way the path now turns."

—John A. Sanford, *Dreams and Healing*

"'We begin with a few threads,' the psychiatrist explained, 'sometimes quite slender and easily broken. But we keep hold as best we can, and we keep weaving, weaving, weaving, creating a stronger and stronger cloth of relationships. It becomes a beautiful tapestry, telling a beautiful story.'"

—Craig Rennebohm with David Paul,
Souls in the Hands of a Tender God,
Stories of the Search for Home and Healing on the Streets

REFLECTION

Have major events in your life affected you significantly or changed your life path?

What is your story? How would you describe your tapestry? Do you admire it? Are you trying to recreate it? Do you feel you wove it together yourself or was it the result of people and events you had no control over?

The Kiss of My Angel

The kiss of my angel still touches my soul! While in her tender embrace, the warmth of her skin against mine makes me pause and stops me in the moment. Her kiss reminds me how blessed I am!

My angel calls my attention to simple things—the important things I need to appreciate in this life. She reminds me,

"This world is only temporary and way out of control."

My angel points out that many unimportant things occupy my existence. When my life is overtaken with rush, chaos, and daily hustle, she reminds me again,

"There is more to life and more to come!
Slow down!
Stay grounded!
Become focused on Godly things!
Discover and remember what is important.
If it fits into God's plan and purpose,
you know it is important if He grants enough time to complete it!
Everything else is only business and busy-ness.
If you feel overburdened, these things only fill time and steal time,
taking time away from what is most important—
your relationship with Our Father,
your family, and His beloved people!"

Even though my angel has gone before me, she still remembers me and loves me ever so much. Memories of her tender embrace make me smile through my tears. I still feel the kiss of my angel, I still hear her words of wisdom, and she still touches my soul!

"What if the answers to our questions about life and path and practice are already speaking to us, and in our rush to find them elsewhere, we miss the easy, gentle wisdom that would teach us all what we need to know if we simply center ourselves and be still for just a moment? And so we are given a commandment: Remember the Sabbath. Rest is an essential enzyme of life, as necessary as air. Without rest, we cannot sustain the energy needed to have life. We refuse to rest at our peril—and yet, in a world where overwork is seen as a professional virtue, many of us feel we can legitimately be stopped only by physical illness or collapse. If we do not allow for a rhythm of rest in our overly busy lives, illness becomes our Sabbath—our pneumonia, our cancer, our heart attack ... our accidents create Sabbath for us. In my relationships with people suffering with cancer, AIDS, and other life-threatening illness, I am always struck by the mixture of sadness and relief they experience when illness interrupts their overly busy lives. While each shares their particular fears and sorrows, almost every one confesses some secret of gratefulness. 'Finally,' they say, 'at last. I can rest.'"

—Wayne Muller, *Sabbath*

REFLECTION

This is how my dearest friend and angel, Shirley Wuerth, was with me: tender, loving, caring, concerned, and watchful. She wanted to protect me, and she watched over me. She tried to warn me when I was neglecting what was important in God's eyes. Though time and space separate us, she still embraces me, she still communicates with me, and still loves me. My angel still blesses my soul!

Have you found yourself so busy you feel like you are missing important things in life? How would your life change if you had more time and let go of things and activities that are not important in God's eyes?

Do you see or look for blessings every day through people or things that remind you of God or a kiss from an angel? Do you reach out to others when you know you could provide *the kiss* they need?

My Discovery

As time passes, some things change and some don't.
Was I missing something? Had I lost all hope?
Was there a missing link that was holding me back?
Why couldn't I discover what it was I thought I lacked?

I searched and searched and tried to learn, but at times, not so well;
many times my life on Earth was a vision of living hell.
Satan was the captor; he deceived and he lied!
He said, "You're unworthy! God's abandoned you this time!"

In my mind, I was captive, as if chained to the wall—
down in a dungeon, dark, I felt I lost it all.
Imprisoned, he taunted me; his evil intention destroyed my dreams.
Then he locked me up within my mind and threw away the keys.

Satan repeatedly deceived me, distorted truth and twisted facts—
he blinded me in darkness; I couldn't see or find God's path.
I heard destructive messages, those meant to crush my soul …
to break me down so I'd give in, letting Satan take control.

Corrupting thoughts and dark shadows Satan placed in my sight,
then promised me a life of joy, if I'd *give up* my fight.
His power became obsessive; damaging shame, he placed on me,
but I fought with all I had to break his grasp on me.

I desperately prayed for Heaven's light of love to shine.
Seeking God's assurance, I'd be saved—I'd be alive!
Holding onto His promise, I cried out, "Save me, Lord!"
He reached out and took my hand and saved my life once more!

He shined His light before me. He showed me why He cared.
He knelt down right beside me and whispered in my ear,
"In My eyes, you are so beautiful, and you are worth the fight;
I'll protect you from evil and remove his terror from your sight!"

God broke Satan's grasp on me—won fierce battles against wrong!
He helped me make some changes and helped guide me along.
With God's strength, I am stronger, but even when I'm not,
I know He is here beside me; for my soul, He has fought!

With God's gift of hope, I smiled when He looked into my eyes,
"I've granted you My holy peace. I know you will survive.
I've healed your body, mind, and soul; you have no need to fear.
I've granted you great strength and faith—
I'll spare your life from here!"

Satan does still tempt me, hoping he will destroy my soul,
but God says, *"You are worthy! I won't allow him any more!"*
God removed the cross I carried—the shame of Satan's grasp.
While in His arms and His embrace,
God says, *"You're mine, at last!"*

At times, I still do struggle; feeling sane, I know I've lacked,
but when I prayed and sought my Lord,
He claimed my soul right back!
God blessed me with His mercy, and I am thankful for my life.
He has taught me to be grateful for all things, even strife!

Created by Our Father, in His image, He made me!
God repeats, *"I'll always love you; within you, you'll find Me!"*
In my discovery, I have learned to trust, and I do believe,
God is my Lord and Savior, and His love sets me free!

"What, then, shall we say in response to this? If God is for us, who can be against us? He who did not spare his own Son, but gave him up for us all—how will he not also, along with him, graciously give us all things? Who will bring any charge against those whom God has chosen? It is God who justifies. Who is he that condemns? Christ Jesus, who died—more than that, who was raised to life—is at the right hand of God and is also interceding for us. Who shall separate us from the love of Christ? For I am convinced that neither death nor life, neither angels nor demons, neither the present nor the future, nor any powers, neither height nor depth, nor anything else in all creation, will be able to separate us from the love of God that is in Christ Jesus our Lord."

—Romans 8:31–39

"When these times of mystery seem endless and our souls become weary of the stretch to believe, our prayer must be a simple request—that we be reminded that we have not been abandoned in this place to wander forever alone ... for it is often a flicker in our heart, the tiny voice within, that whispers wordlessly, 'You are always loved. You are never alone.'"

—Doris Klein, *The Journey of the Soul*

REFLECTION

Almost more than I could bear, I learned firsthand how conniving evil people could be, hell-bent on destroying whoever questioned their power, threatened their authority, or refused to be submissive. God's intervention was the only thing that saved me, rescuing me from Satan's grasp, protecting me from further harm.

Have you ever felt as though Satan was holding you captive, that an encounter with someone evil had control of your life, intentionally making your life miserable or unbearable?

Have you ever felt someone was overpowering your mind, forcing his or her will upon you, trying to break you down? How have you dealt with it? Are you still struggling or have you broken away from the situation?

He Blessed Me Abundantly

Near the end of my day, as the twilight of dusk disappeared, I joined God in the quiet stillness of my room. His presence entered my awareness as I cleared my mind so I could hear Him when He spoke to me.

A quick strike from a matchbook sparked a flame, and I lit a candle that illuminated my space in His midst. Its gentle glow cast soft shadows within my room and flickering reflections from a mirror multiplied its wavering illumination. The small flame captivated me and helped me focus as its light gradually penetrated dark recesses of my mind, allowing me to see through God's eyes.

I began by giving thanks for this quiet, intimate moment with God, and then I recalled the path I walked throughout my day. I delighted as He revealed His presence, showing me how He wove Himself in and out of my consciousness since this morning's sunrise. My spirit lifted when I saw how often He interrupted my concentration long enough to give me a reprieve from my escalating stress. I smiled while listening to several melodic tunes, lyrical phrases, and chanting Psalms, remembering they gladdened my heart every time they resonated within me. And then, my Lord whispered, *"These were just a few gentle reminders that My Spirit is alive and moving within you."*

God continued revealing specific people He intentionally placed before me during the day. I heard their voices and remembered everyone who touched my heart with their soul, how their kindness and compassion spoke to me. Entrusting me with part of their story, some simply needed someone to listen and acknowledge their current concerns. I offered encouragement, hoping to touch their heart and soul with words of God's truth and sincerity, hoping they heard Christ speaking from within my heart. God imparted His gracious gift of peace, and He smiled as He watched me trying to follow His example of comforting and soothing words to ease their pain and turmoil.

When God shifted my state of awareness, He revealed His insight to my thoughts throughout my day. He replayed conversations within my mind, pointing out things I had said, thoughts that had crossed my mind, and opinions I had that were not pleasing to Him. His keen observation stunned me, because many of my thoughts were unconscious. He addressed them, one at a time, graciously pointing out distorted facts and minor misconceptions. He exposed Satan's deceit that was beginning to gnaw at my consciousness, intentionally causing me to doubt. While Satan hoped I'd lose my way and sense of self-worth, God continued working His grace in my mind and soul.

Lovingly, God enlightened me with different ways of expressing things I could say and how He hoped I would respond next time. He instructed me, *"Turn your thoughts to Me, so I may guide and direct you. You are My joy and My delight. You are My hope to make this world a better place.*

"Every day, I think of you as precious and amazing, especially when I see what you go through! Before I can help you, you must give it all up and surrender your control. You will need to relinquish every injustice, everything that frustrates you, especially for children, because you know life does not need to be so difficult for the little ones."

Continuing to reassure and encourage me, He repeated what He had often told me, *"I am here! I am always with you and by your side. I only need to hear you call My name and I will step forward and help you, but I will not interfere when it is a result or consequence of your choices. I will allow you to make your own decisions, even your own mistakes, because this is how you will learn.*

"I can heal your troubled heart and lift burdens that weigh you down.

I will restore your strength and provide you enough energy for what is important. When you begin to feel apprehensive, question Me. I will have every answer you need! I delight in bringing you hope for a better tomorrow. I assure you, My pain and suffering was worth it; your pain and suffering will be worth it, too!"

Returning my consciousness to this world, He brought my focus back to His Spirit dancing within the flickering light. In my mind, He restored peacefulness and calmed my anxiety. He eased the disappointments that disturbed my soul, and He blocked the anxiousness that Satan had attempted to use to confuse me and steal my joy.

Once again, fully aware of the quiet stillness that surrounded me, I inhaled and pondered God's words. I smiled, acknowledging His affirming passionate love, and He smiled, too, then He blessed me abundantly, *"In the name of the Father, and the Son, and the Holy Spirit. Amen!"*

"The gift of the threshold provides a way to cross over into a fuller life of spiritual depth and freedom. When we choose to traverse the invisible boundary of the known self and enter the unknown, we are saying: 'Yes, I want to grow, to become wiser, to be strengthened, to be less burdened by what weighs me down and keeps me from being my authentic self. I am willing to pay the price of this growth.'"

—Joyce Rupp, *Open the Door, A Journey to the True Self*

REFLECTION

Even though I know the depth of my faith, and I know I trust God, I have barely endured emotional devastation that wounds my soul. Personally, I experience heartache, separation, and death with overwhelming grief. There have been times when I was left to question whether I would survive, whether I would ever feel love, peace, and joy again.

God knows the internal agony I have experienced and He gives me hope! He repeatedly promises He will protect my heart and soul. He leads me through every moment when I am unstable, and He helps me clearly see through His eyes. He is pleased to see I have not given up, and He blesses me abundantly!

Have you experienced a separation from someone you loved deeply? What caused your separation or loss … was it death, a broken relationship, a divorce, loss of a job, financial security, your health, or the health of a loved one, etc.? If you have experienced any loss, do you ever wonder if you will survive? What helps you know you were or are going to be okay?

"The gift of the threshold …" What price are you willing to pay, or rather, what are you willing to sacrifice or give up in order to become wiser and less burdened? Was there an event or were there several events in your life that headed you toward the threshold? Have you crossed over yet? Do you think you have finally arrived?

PART FIVE

Encouragement and Hope

"Without seeing you, we love you;
without touching you, we embrace;
without knowing you, we follow;
without seeing you, we believe!"

DAVID HAAS, *Without Seeing You*

A Voice of Reassurance

Be patient! In time, you will wonder why you ever allowed this struggle to cause you so much distress! Trust Me. I have a plan for whatever comes, regardless what you decide to do. You know I can free you from feeling caught in webs of doubt and fear, but Satan will use everything he can to harm you when he can't maintain power or control over you. I know he will discourage you and make you doubt yourself; he will attempt to lead you to doubt Me. I know he will try to wear you down, but if he wants revenge, he will try to destroy you.

Come, walk with Me and leave this struggle behind. Walk with Me to the meadow beyond the woods, where the breeze of the day and sounds of nature envelop you.

Come, follow Me as we climb to the top of the hill, where you can see far and the sky is endless.

Sit here and rest with Me. Breathe in all that is pure; allow it to cleanse and refresh your soul. Exhale all that troubles you; let all distress flow out of you. Allow Me to calm your anxiousness and ease your suffering. Allow Me to nurture you back to wholeness.

Relax. I want you to remember this place and keep it safe within your mind and soul. You can come here as often as you need, and you will find Me here! I will restore you every time you seek Me for guidance, love, and protection.

Come now, follow Me down the backside of the hill where it levels off and gradually slopes into the valley. At the bottom, sounds of the stream and birds will be the only sounds you hear.

Stop, be still, and listen. Close your eyes and allow me to nourish you and give you My strength to continue and go on. Allow wonders of My creation to bless you and bring you peace of mind.

Be thankful for the journey I have chosen for your life. I will lead you through to a victorious outcome. No matter what is yet to come, do not be *afraid! I will not leave you or abandon you. One day, you will understand your journey and the meaning of your life.*

Make a difference in this world! Be thankful for each person I have placed on your path; they are meant for you to love and forgive, to teach and learn from, to hold and let go. Use and share what I have blessed you with to make a difference in their lives. Love those I have brought into your life, and love them with all your heart. Cherish each moment with them because time on Earth is limited. There will be blessings for both of you, but some opportunities only come once in your lifetime.

Be grateful for each day that I, the Lord, have made for you! Be humble because today is the only day that matters. Each and every moment right now is priceless! Don't worry about tomorrow; I have tomorrow taken care of.

I love you! Always and forever, God

"How near can we draw to Him when we pray? Near enough to speak a whisper and still be clearly heard; near enough to know that every sigh is understood; near enough to be assured that even the deepest prayer that the heart cannot put into words is fully known."

—Roy Lessin,
meetmeinthemeadow.com/2013/06/promises-on-prayer

REFLECTION

Have you ever awakened in the night from a startling dream or felt an urgent sense of fear overtake you, even if it was fear of the unknown? Do you pray relentlessly when discontentment, disappointment, or fear enters your life? Do you seek reassurance? Do you ask for wisdom and guidance, for hope and relief, for love and forgiveness?

Has someone turned to you seeking reassurance when something happened to them? How do you reassure them? Do you pray together? Have you suggested professional or spiritual guidance?

Someone is Waiting for You

Be patient and believe! I have chosen someone who is waiting for you!

I hear your prayers, asking for a loving relationship. I know you are lonely, longing for someone to love and love you back, but this is part of My plan. I am preparing you for a most loving relationship, and I will decide when you are ready to move on. In the meantime, you have lessons to learn during your time alone. You need time to discover more about yourself and your relationship with Me.

Along the way, I will send you messages and assure you with My Word. Listen for My voice! Seek Me to satisfy your deepest desires! In time, you will believe I only want the very best for you. I want you to understand the depth of My love. I want you to feel My guiding hand protect you from further heartache and pain, from grief and loss.

The one I have chosen for you will live according to My plan. He will be compassionate and sincere, warm and affectionate. He will be your true and lasting love, and you will be his. He will have longed for you, as much as you have longed for him!

When you finally come together, you will know you were meant for each other. As you begin to know him, you will discover you have crossed the same territory. Even though you have traveled separate journeys, you will recognize you have walked many of the same paths—some in the same direction, some from the opposite direction.

Once you have arrived, you will understand why this journey was necessary and important. You will trust My judgment and be grateful for every lesson you have learned. Together, you will respect and honor each other, love and nurture each other. You will walk side by side and hand in hand. You will stand before Me and begin a new life together!

Trust Me! I have someone waiting for someone just like you!

"To love means loving the unlovable. To forgive means pardoning the unpardonable. Faith means believing the unbelievable. Hope means hoping when everything seems hopeless. Hope is the power of being cheerful in circumstances that we know to be desperate. Happiness is not only a hope, but also in some strange manner a memory. There is the great lesson in *Beauty and the Beast*, that a thing must be loved before it is lovable. Love is not blind; that is the last thing it is. Love is bound; and the more it is bound the less it is blind."

—G. K. Chesterton from *A Chestertonian Thanksgiving* by Darrin Moore, November 22, 2012

"I do not believe that sheer suffering teaches. If suffering alone taught, all the world would be wise, since everyone suffers. To suffering must be added mourning, understanding, patience, love, openness, and the willingness to remain vulnerable."

—Anne Morrow Lindbergh, *Gift From the Sea*

REFLECTION

While in the presence of a dear friend who was devastated by the loss of her husband, God spoke these words for me to share with her. More and more often, God moved my heart to help me show His compassion to others who were experiencing so much pain and agony. As I listened to her share her struggle, God instilled His words in me to encourage her and give her hope for love once again.

Have you ever longed for the return of the love you lost? Did you believe what you lost in that relationship could return to you through someone else, or something completely different, such as your church, volunteering, or offering yourself to be of loving service to others?

What was your greatest life trial? How did you survive? Have you given hope to someone who is struggling with a similar loss? If so, how?

Standing Still

Standing still in complete darkness, suspended in time and space, I was barely able to survive since the one I dearly loved had died. There was nowhere to escape, nowhere to hide. Reality overcame me in a moment, swinging the pendulum from one state of mind to another, from being entranced, emotionless, and locked inside myself to crying out of control.

As my tears flowed, I couldn't seem to stop them any more than I could have stopped a flooding riverbank. Like rising waters that begin to swell, swirling at every bend, my tears whisked me away and prevented me from being able to regain any sense of being grounded. Relentless torrents pursued me and weakened me, wearing down every layer of strength and sanity I had. I felt as though my life was beyond the point of no return.

Caught in life's grasp, desperate for relief while gasping for air, I was mentally and emotionally exhausted. I rarely experienced a moment to catch my breath before I was swept downstream and further away. I longed for my life as it used to be, and yet, I knew I would never be the same again.

Even though I knew it was coming, I was not prepared for the loneliness that consumed me, but then, how could anyone prepare for losing someone they loved? I was not prepared for losing my ability to think and remember. I was not prepared for the possibility of losing my mind or feeling as if I already had.

Within each conscious moment, I prayed for a way out of my darkness and intensifying grief. I yearned for the return of peace and tranquility, to feel whole and well. I closed my eyes, trying to shield myself from what I had no control over. I couldn't bear my deep sadness, and I was afraid I might not survive. I longed to find a place to rest my raging mind, a place of shelter from the storm within, but I couldn't escape.

Still being swept away, I continued to pray for a sign of hope. I longed for His voice of reassurance to know moments of Heaven on Earth would return once again in my lifetime.

When I finally opened my eyes, I saw the light of God's presence. Instantly, I knew I was within the realm of His gracious love. He was in my midst—He had come back for *me*! He immediately eased my pain and restored my ability to think and comprehend. He waited patiently for me to reach out to take His hand, and He rescued me by pulling me out of the depths I was drowning in.

Holding me still, God's embrace calmed my soul; the feeling of being out of control faded away. His infinite capacity for compassion acknowledged my pain and accepted my broken spirit. He continued to surround me with His healing power, warmth, and overwhelming love, and I was so grateful … I was so relieved!

Before I realized how much time had passed, I discovered my renewed consciousness was effortless. Peace and contentment over-flowed from my soul once again, as God allowed me to look back and see where I had been. Together, we reviewed everything I had been through and everything I had survived. I could actually see how far I had already journeyed, and I no longer heard cascades of confusion and rushing sounds of ongoing agony—they had all faded away!

When I thanked God for rescuing me and restoring my hope, He immediately promised, *"You will always find refuge and endure this life while living in My presence … all you need to do is trust your life with Me!"*

As time continued to pass, God sustained His promise! He show-ered me with blessings of grace and mercy; He protected me with His mighty strength and power; He maintained my footing when I walked by His side; He blessed me when I sought and followed His direction. I acknowledged God in my thoughts and prayer, gave Him all glory, honor, and praise, and then I realized I was no longer *standing still*!

"Save me, God, for the waters have reached my neck! I have sunk into the mire of the deep, where there is no foothold. I have gone down to the watery depths; the flood overwhelms me. I am weary with crying out; my throat is parched. My eyes have failed, looking for my God."

—Psalm 69:2–4

"I want to share these loving, powerful words written by my friend and medical school classmate, Dr. Walter Menninger, that I think are so important for all survivors to remember—'Learn to read your own signals that the limits are being approached or gone beyond. Be comfortable in asking for help when your limits are surpassed.'"

—Bernie Siegel,
May It Never Be Again—Reflections on 9/11/2001

REFLECTION

While participating in my third Hospice Grief Recovery Program, uncontrollable feelings swept over me and carried me away. My life was out of control again. All of our lives seemed out of control, but each one of us had made another step in the right direction. As we continued to seek understanding and relief from our losses, we were able to support each other. We were able to help save each other.

Have you ever felt as though you were being swept away, caught in the current, unable to stop the driving force of helplessness, even hopelessness? Do you know what caused that feeling? Was it a death, a terminal diagnosis, loss of your own health, or an unraveling relationship? Was it being disabled, ongoing unemployment, or recently losing your job? Is it your own self-destructive behavior or "losing your mind"?

If you are in the midst of standing still or being swept away, can you shift or stop the momentum? Do you know what you need to do or who to ask for help to save you from your block wall or downward spiral? Have you been able to return to a sense of normalcy? What did you learn about yourself during and/or after your struggle?

My Lost and Found Vision

I had lost my vision and couldn't find my way.
Confusion in my life and mind took my sight away.
I couldn't see my future because I was so lost.
With broken heart and yearning soul, I longed for whom I lost.

God entered in my darkness, granting light for me to see.
He had a plan and vision, many hopes and dreams for me!
Even though I had my sight, I was blind in other ways.
God told me, *"You are worth the price; I'll save you every day!"*

He told me how He loved me, and then He prayed with me.
"I have faith in who you are, just turn and follow Me."
He blessed me through His people, all those who followed Him;
He sent them back to capture me and lead me back to Him.

"People helping people is what this world's about."
Then I remembered those He sent, and now I have no doubt!
*"I know you know what you should do—for someone else, reach out!
This life's not all about you; helping others will help you out!*

*"And don't forget your future. I have plans and dreams for you.
I've chosen you to do My work, to save someone like you.
In My plan, you'll share your journey, being lost and found,
and I will help you see and know, your lost soul has been found.*

"When you share your story, let them know I long for them.
When troubled and downhearted, if they ask, I'll come for them."
Now I believe in who I am and who I'm meant to be.
With God's plan and purpose for my life, He saved and set me free!

"So in pain, confusion, or indifference, with clarity, conviction, or a 'Who cares?' shrug, those who struggle step back a step into the margins. For many, it is a life-giving move. There, they meet others who have been ignored, diminished, and belittled. There, the reassurance of the marginal community sounds clear: 'You're not alone, and you're not crazy.' That message may even be phrased as the elegant invitation of the adage: 'As long as we're walking on thin ice, we might as well dance!' In God's steady arms, we rejuvenate, transform, heal, and try a few wobbly dance steps. Within the circle of God's embrace, we hear beneath the surface cacophony as lovely music. God calls us to plunge deeper and to move on gracefully."

—Kathy Coffey, *Dancing in the Margins*

"To be lonely is to feel unwanted and unloved, and therefore unlovable. Loneliness is a taste of death. No wonder some people who are desperately lonely lose themselves in mental illness or violence to forget the inner pain."

—Jean Vanier, *Becoming Human*

REFLECTION

Have you found yourself in the margins? If so, were you placed there intentionally by someone else? Did you stay in the margins long or were you able to move yourself back into the mainstream? Were you humbled? What did you learn from an experience of being "pushed out" or "shut out"?

Did you find yourself closer to God while you were in the margins? Were you amazed when you realized how many other people were in the margins and they chose to stay? Were many able to find their true self and then move on?

Have you ever moved someone into the margins, out of your way? Did you ever look back, go back, or apologize to them? Were you strong enough or humble enough to do what you knew you needed to do to make it right with them?

An Angel of God

An angel of God held out her hand
and led me to a quiet place, unplanned.
She sat with me and held me close,
saying, *"I really care, but God loves you the most!"*

She comforted me and dried my tears,
"I've been with you already for so many years.
God knows you've been lonely and experienced great pain,
but please, be patient. It'll ease like the rain!

"His Master Plan and visions for you
are full of great things He hopes for you!
He wants you to feel His presence and love,
that is why I've been sent to you from above.

"Angels, like friends, are here, and you'll see …
to comfort and hold you whenever you need.
I'll always be close and with tender heart,
I'll show you His ways to find love in your heart.

"I am one of God's angels sent to you from above,
to guide and to show you His never-ending love!"

"Then he said to me, 'Do not be afraid, Daniel, for from the first day that you set your heart on understanding this and on humbling yourself before your God, your words were heard, and I have come in response to your words.'"
—Daniel 10:12–13

"The feeling remains that God is on the journey, too."
—Saint Teresa of Avila, *Wisdom of the Heart*

REFLECTION

Have you ever felt the presence of an angel leading you? Did someone come in the appearance of a friend, or was someone sent to comfort you and you knew God had sent him or her? What did they tell you? Did they deliver a message from God?

If you have an angel, have they told you God's truth—whatever God wanted you to hear? Was it someone whose presence was all you needed? Is your angel someone who always makes you feel unconditionally loved?

God's Voice of Hope

God's voice of hope encourages me to never give up. *"There is always hope!"* He reassures me to trust and believe—He is the one and only Holy and just God! He inspires me to continue to believe in myself, because He believes in me. He dares me to remember "who I am" and discover "who I am" meant to be.

God's voice of hope gives me strength to endure and persevere. He guides me to find purpose in this life and grants me visions of Everlasting Life! He urges me to be patient, asking me to follow where He leads. He directs me onward through life and commands me, *"Stop looking back!"*

God's voice of hope guides my thoughts and explains the depths of my soul. He offers insight when I pray, providing a greater understanding of my life. He reinforces my hope and He persuades me to follow my dreams and listen with my heart.

God's voice of hope helps me refocus when I am feeling lost, lonely, and insecure. He quiets voices of ruthlessness to protect my heart and soul. He grants me divine peace and contentment in His presence. He blesses my existence and tells me, *"You are My Beloved!"*

God's voice of hope sings softly to soothe my soul and bring me into His presence. He chants ageless wisdom and shares His wealth of knowledge. He promises He will love me forever and fills my heart with compassion for others. He presents opportunities for me to reach out to comfort them, to help them understand their own life trials.

God's voice of hope echoes with authority, making sure I know His power! He speaks to me in the silence, comforting me when I least expect it; He whispers affirming words to lift my spirits, casting my doubts away. With kindness, He reminds me how much He cares for me. He expresses His unconditional love and mercy, urging me: *"Be a living testimony that I am alive within you! Never be afraid to acknowledge you are who you are. Never be afraid to show others My place in your life. Never be afraid to share what I have done for you."*

God's voice of hope humbles my earthly awareness and calms my yearning heart. He reveals my place in this world, so I will understand what is important. I will always listen for the voice of God because God's voice is *a voice of hope*!

"For I know well the plans I have in mind for you, says the LORD, plans for your welfare, not for woe; plans to give you a future full of hope."
—Jeremiah 29:11

"Therefore, I, too, hearing of your faith in the Lord Jesus and of your love for all the holy ones, do not cease giving thanks for you, remembering you in my prayers, that the God of our Lord Jesus Christ, the Father of glory, may give you a spirit of wisdom and revelation resulting in knowledge of him."
—Ephesians 1:15–17

"Let us hold unwaveringly to our confession that gives us hope, for he who made the promise is trustworthy. We must consider how to rouse one another to love and good works."
—Hebrews 10:23–24

REFLECTION

Have you heard *a voice of hope* speaking to you in a dream? Was there a message? If so, have you shared the message with others?

Has anyone ever conveyed to you that they heard *a voice* or *the voice of God*? Did they share what *the voice* said to them? If so, how did you react or respond? Did you believe them?

Somewhere Deep Within

Somewhere deep within is a baby girl
who longs to be swaddled and feel secure.
She longs to feel her parents' love and God's love.
She longs to be fed, kept dry, and to see your smile.
She longs to know everything in her newborn world
is going to be okay.

Somewhere deep within is a little girl
who begins to ask about God's love.
She longs to have fun and feel secure.
She longs for her parents' love while learning about God's love.
She longs to be loved by siblings and extended family.
She longs to be accepted and know she belongs.
She longs to know everything in her young family world
is going to be okay.

Somewhere deep within is a young woman
who longs to discover love and feel secure.
She longs to feel her friend's love and witness God's love.
She longs to find a young man who might like her.
She longs for the first date with the man of her dreams.
She longs to fall in love with the man she'll love forever.
She longs for a commitment and wants to help others.
She longs to know everything in her young-woman world
is going to be okay.

Somewhere deep within is a young wife
who longs to be loved and feel secure.
She longs to live with her beloved "until death do us part."
She longs to feel her husband's love and know God's love.
She longs to know he will protect her.
She longs to be cherished in a place they call home.
She longs for God's wisdom and direction in her marriage.
She longs for unconditional love from her husband.
She longs to understand forgiveness is a gift,
but knows it won't be easy.
She longs to know everything in her married world
is going to be okay.

Somewhere deep within is a new mother
who longs to love every miracle of life God blesses her with.
She longs to feel her babies' love and know it's God's love.
She longs to embrace and cradle, to rock and nurture her children.
She longs to encourage them to believe and walk with God.
She longs for a restful night's sleep, but knows she will endure.
She longs to know everything in her family world
is going to be okay.

Somewhere deep within is a new grandmother
who longs to share her love beyond measure with her grandchildren.
She longs to feel worthy of little ones' love and God's love.
She longs to embrace and nurture them and be a part of their lives.
She longs to know they will have a good, safe, and secure life.
She longs to hear their voices tell their own stories.

She longs to watch them grow and see them learn.
She longs to have them visit and spend the night.
She longs to teach them to bake and sew and play games together.
She longs to know her next-generation world
is going to be okay.

Somewhere deep within is an old woman
who experienced love and understood life.
She raised and loved her children and grandchildren.
She shared stories of her past with others and her loved ones.
She was blessed by love of her friends, family, and God.
She struggled from time to time with loneliness.
She prayed and began thinking about her Heavenly Home.
She always had hope and believed in God's Divine Mercy.
She believed God was in control and trusted in His timing.
She thanked God for dreams, life lessons, and opportunities.
She gave away her possessions to share a part of herself with others.
She knew everything in her aging world
was going to be okay.

Somewhere deep within are memories of her.
We remember how much she loved life and all of us.
We remember what she told us and taught us to believe.
We remember how she blessed us and gave us hope.
We remember she always believed everything in her life
was going to be okay!

"At dawn let me hear of your kindness, for in you I trust. Show me the path I should walk, for to you I entrust my life. Teach me to do your will, for you are my God. May your kind spirit guide me on ground that is level."

—Psalm 143:8, 10

"In order to be a teacher of peace, one must first of all nurture peace within."

—Pope John Paul II. *Spiritual Advice from John Paul II*, compiled by Mary Emmanuel Alves and Molly H. Rosa

"The key to faith is love. We believe only if we love. Trust is the middle term; only if we love, do we trust; and only if we trust, do we believe."

—Peter Kreeft, *The God Who Loves You*

REFLECTION

Somewhere deep within, each of us carries memories of who we once were. May you be blessed by living your life well, and may your life touch others and bless them.

Looking back over your entire life journey, do you remember and still recognize the person you once were? Whatever age you were then or whatever age you are now, do you still yearn to be loved?

As you age, do you find yourself wiser—granted more wisdom and knowledge—more accepting and patient with God in your life? Do you have more to learn?

PART SIX

In His Presence

"Deep within, I will plant my law,
Not on stone, but in your heart.
Follow me; I will bring you back.
You will be my own, and I will be your God."

DAVID HAAS, *Deep Within*

For a Reason

Everything happens for a reason.

God knew this moment was meant to be. He knew there was a place for this moment in the realm of His kingdom. He knew before we were born, and He already had our destiny planned.

God knew our parents before we were conceived. He knew when and where we would be born. He knew every relative, friend, and foe we would encounter. He knew our life before it unfolded. He already knew our lifespan on Earth!

God knew we needed to know what is righteous and unrighteous. He knew our reasoning behind each decision we would make. He knew the pain our choices and consequences would cause us. He knew we would learn lessons an easy way or the hard way. He knew He would always accept us and forgive us. He already knew how much He loved us!

God knew every thought and feeling we would have within us. He knew we needed to learn who we were meant to be. He knew we needed to discover our need for others in our lives. He knew we needed to help and serve the poorest of the poor. He knew we would realize something was missing in our lives. He already knew we would need Him and seek Him!

God knew He needed to watch over us, to pray for us, and to pray with us. He knew who would nurture us and who would devastate us. He knew true love would bring joy; death would bring sorrow. He knew we would encounter trials that would challenge us. He knew battles would be fierce, and wounds would weaken us. He knew our strength and hope would become compromised. He already knew he would need to fight for us, protect us, and save us from harm.

God knew every fork in the road our life journeys would come to. He knew the directions we'd choose and the mistakes we'd make. He knew our decisions would determine the lessons we'd learn. He knew we could get lost and need help finding our way. He knew He would walk with us and rescue us, whether we asked for His help or not. He already knew the outcome of our journeys!

Everything happens for a reason.

"My Lord God, I have no idea where I am going, I do not see the road ahead of me, I cannot know for certain where it will end. Nor do I really know myself, and the fact that I think I am following your will does not mean that I am actually doing so. But I believe that the desire to please you does in fact please you. And I hope I have that desire in all that I am doing. I hope that I will never do anything apart from that desire. And I know that if I do this, you will lead me by the right road, though I may know nothing about it. Therefore, I will trust you always, though I may seem to be lost and in the shadow of death. I will not fear, for you are ever with me, and you will never leave me to face my perils alone."

—Thomas Merton, *Thoughts in Solitude*

REFLECTION

Have you experienced a fork in the road or a major life decision that changed your life path? Have you regretted what you previously decided or blamed someone else for a life-altering choice you made or you made together?

Have you ever taken another path to escape where you are because your situation or consequences became too difficult to endure? Did God lead you away for your own sake?

Where are you now and where do you want to be? Do you believe you are where God intended you to be? Why or why not?

His Longings and Hopes for You

I long for you to believe My outstretched arms and tears are for you.
I long for you to allow Me to surround you in My loving embrace.
I long for you to experience the depth of My unconditional love.
I hope you know how much I love you, how much I suffered for you.

I long for a full and loving relationship with you every day.
I long for you to seek and spend time with Me in thought and prayer.
I long for your faith to be strengthened in good times and in bad.
I hope you believe My promise of hope and salvation is for you.

I long to hear you call out My name when you feel lost or forsaken.
I long for you to know the way to Everlasting Life is through Me.
I long for you to find your path and acknowledge I chose it for you.
I hope you share your blessings with others along your journey.

I long for you to forgive others and let go of the pain you feel.
I long for you to seek My forgiveness and ask others to forgive you.
I long for you to forgive yourself and move forward in your life.
I hope you allow Me to completely heal your heart and soul.

I long to lift the weight and distress your burdens have caused you.
I long to lighten your load so you may regain your perspective.
I long for you to give up disappointment and discouragement.
I hope you accept My gifts of peace, joy, and contentment in life.

I long to replace all that ails you with My promise of healing.
I long for you to live free from unnecessary suffering and pain.

I long for you to return to Me and let Me carry your crosses for you.
I hope you accept all My love so others may find Me through you.

I long for you to realize I experience every moment of your agony.
I long for you to believe when I say, "I understand your pain."
I long for you to trust and believe I will help you endure and survive.
I hope you know My sacrifice and death was worth the price I paid.

"To love someone is not, first of all, to do things for them, but to reveal to them their beauty and value, to say to them through our attitude: 'You are beautiful. You are important. I trust you. You can trust yourself ...' To love someone is to reveal to them their capacities for life, the light that is shining in them."
—Jean Vanier, *Becoming Human*

"God never forces Himself upon us or works in us beyond what we are willing to allow Him to do. If we do not grow in love, it is not because His love for us is limited, but because we set limits to what His love can do in us."
—Thomas Green, *When the Well Runs Dry*

REFLECTION

God prays for us, always hoping we will find time for Him, longing for us to accept Him into our lives and believe He only wants the best for us.

What do you hope for in life? What do you long for? Have you told God every hope and longing you desire to come true? Do you believe God wants a better life for you? Do you believe in a Heavenly future? Why or why not?

In His Presence

In His presence, I stirred into wakefulness. Keenly aware, I was surrounded by a calming stillness in the early-morning air. The sun had not yet crested the horizon and the birds and squirrels were still silent. Contentment and peacefulness lingered within me, so I closed my eyes to rest a little while longer.

The next time I stirred, the sun had already moved to midday; I must have slept for hours. Out of nowhere, like the swoop of an eagle upon its prey, I found myself mercilessly clenched in the talons of reality; my body had shut down again! Disheartened, I sighed deeply, and then I prayed for God's immediate protection and swift encouragement to help me endure yet another relapse.

Inconceivable exhaustion completely obstructed my ability to ward off an immediate onslaught of irrational, self-defeating thoughts as they began to invade my consciousness. They interfered with my effort and need to pray; they questioned and mocked my faith, trying to destroy my hope. They succeeded in making me believe I was unworthy of anyone's love once again.

I slept a lot, but when I was conscious, I felt as though I was being challenged. I felt as if I had no opinion worth voicing, nothing intelligent to say, and I was nothing but a disappointment to others. Satan had somehow managed to delve into my dreams and tried convincing me God would not forgive a sinner like me because I was undeserving. I blamed myself for the state I was in, and this was my punishment.

Once I succumbed to the unrelenting stronghold that fatigue had placed on my everyday life, I was too weak to withstand the choked feeling in my throat, and I sobbed; tears welled up and spilled from my eyes. I felt God had forsaken me; I instantly lost hope and was giving up on myself. Many of my dreams and thoughts, whether conscious or unconscious, had become one and the same: This was it! I would not recover, and I just had to accept it!

Many times, I was unable to tell if I was asleep or awake, but upon returning from one of my vivid nightmares, I was abruptly awakened when my soul cried out, "Lord, in Your presence, I surrender!"

In the moments that followed, God appeared before me. He pulled me out of the depths I was lost in and silenced the sounds and voices that were overpowering my mind. He gathered up my body, embracing me tightly like cradling an inconsolable, sobbing child. In His presence, my anxiety and despair began to ease. He patiently waited for my weeping gasps to cease and my breathing to return to normal before He began to speak. He reassured me again, as He has done so many times before …

"You know I will take care of you like no one on Earth, but you need to let Me. You need to allow Me to do My work in your life! I have always admired you as My Precious One, and even though you often think you're not, you will always be worthy of My love.

"I am relieved that you have resigned and surrendered the battle you cannot fight on your own. I see how difficult it has been for you, and I know how deeply wounded you have become. I have witnessed your unwavering determination to succeed and overcome difficulty, to carry the load I did not intend you to carry alone.

"I have been watching you give so much of yourself away. I know you're not taking care of your own needs, because you have been taking care of so many others' needs. Even though you know you've been compromising your body, mind, and soul, I won't allow you to keep going at this pace. I am intervening! I am stepping in to take care of you.

"So often, even though you have spent time with me, I have missed you, because you've been so busy and preoccupied. I respect the loving devotion you have to your family and work, as well as those who seek you in other ways, but sometimes, you have a few things out of perspective. And yes, I know they need you and appreciate what you do for them, but for now, you need Me more than they need you! I want you to let Me help you and heal you. You might as well surrender everything, because I won't allow you to take any of it back—not until I see you have learned your lesson and regained your strength. Like it or not, I am in charge of your life and I am changing the direction you are headed!"

Right then, God's Spirit lifted the weight from my weary body. In a soft whisper, He continued, *"Deep inside, you know what you need to do at this very moment in your life. Do not be afraid; take that step! I have so much more planned for you, but you need to trust Me.*

"*I do know what is best for you! I am sorry you feel you have let others down, that you have even let yourself down, but I am not sorry that you cannot continue to do this on your own anymore! This is not a sign of failure or weakness, but an incredible testimony of your faith and trust in Me.*

"*When I created you, it was My plan to be close to you, always and forever! I never wanted you to think you had to do it all or think you didn't need My help. I never expected you to place so much importance on your worldly circumstances or your job; so My heart is delighted to see you know how much you need Me now. Even though you sometimes forget to trust Me, I don't mind reminding you from time to time.*"

I was stunned by His commanding, firm manner of scolding me. He interrupted my thoughts when He spoke again, "*Starting with your loving relationships and your joy. Oh, but I've noticed, you haven't had true joy for a long, long time! And I want you to give Me all your pain and grief, everything that has disturbed your peace of mind, everything that weighs heavy on your heart, everything that feels burdensome. Once you have totally surrendered, I will be able to ease your burden and lift its yoke from your shoulders. By letting everything else go, you will create the space in your heart and soul that can truly accept My gifts of love and mercy.*

"*I know you feel beaten down, as though you have lost another great battle, but I am the strength and power you need. Allow Me to step back in and show you how much you mean to Me. No matter what other people say, you deserve everything I grant you. Every blessing and joy I bestow upon you is yours to accept, not to question.*

"*I am the One who can heal your broken heart, the One who can heal your mind and body connection. I have waited for this moment, for just enough space in your confused mind and weary soul for you to let Me back in. Let Me do this for you!*"

I continued to listen as God spoke clearly, "*In My eyes, you are My Beloved Daughter. I have given you as much time as you felt you needed, until today! I have followed your footsteps, but now, I am going to carry you, because you need to feel secure. Place your total trust in Me; I will not let you down! Accept My Word as your truth! I am the living bread, come down from Heaven. I am the life-giving food for your soul! I will sustain you, keep you, and take care of you! I will help you recover!*

"As long as necessary, I will continue to carry you, renew your strength, restore your mind, and show you the only way forward is through Me! Rest in My arms as long as you need, because I have waited a long time for you! Like a mother waits to hold her newborn child, I could hold you forever, but My hope and prayer for you is that you will walk on your own soon enough and be by My side!"

In God's embrace, this moment was heavenly. I wondered why I had held out so long. Why was I so afraid to do what I knew I needed to do? God leaned away from me slightly, looked in my eyes, and He smiled! Knowing my exact thoughts, He wondered, too. Shaking His head, He snickered at me lovingly, and then, He allowed me to settle again in His arms, assuring me, *"Everything is going to be okay."*

Once I had enough courage, I talked openly with God. He listened and heard every word I said. As tired and exhausted as I was, I began to drift off. He gently nudged me, bringing my consciousness back to Him; then, in His mighty wisdom, He simply said, *"Shall we pray?"*

"My Lord and Savior, I seek Your Holy Wisdom and understanding; may I clearly see and follow Your path. You say I am worthy, but I feel unworthy. Help me feel worthy to be healed, and may my pain be a symbol of sacrifice for my faith and belief in You. When worldly things smother me, please fill my heart and soul with Your encouragement to know I can endure for Your name's sake when I place my complete trust in You.

"Please fuel my yearning with the flames of Your Spirit, so I may always see Your light and feel the warmth of Your love within me. Please grant me an unwavering peace of mind in Your presence; please grant me restorative rest and reaffirm my hope in You."

At that moment, God interrupted me and tipped my head upward so He could gaze into my eyes. He knew when He had my attention, but He wanted to see that I actually understood what He was about to say. With His heartfelt love and belief in me, He spoke these words of hope for my future: *"I want your life to be different! I want you to be a living example of hope and love for everyone who walks into your life! I want them to see you have survived because of Me!"*

Beaming with inexplicable joy, I believed I am His Chosen One, His Beloved Daughter. He filled my heart and soul with His overwhelming love. He granted me patience and restored my health. And then, He blessed me: *"In the name of the Father, and the Son, and the Holy Spirit. Amen!"* In that moment, I knew I would never need to question Him again. God has fulfilled His promises to me, and He continues to heal me in His presence. I have survived by the grace of God!

"Though I walk in the midst of dangers, you guard my life when my enemies rage; you stretch out your hand; your right hand saves me. The LORD is with me to the end. LORD, your love endures forever. Never forsake the work of your hands!"
—Psalm 138:7–8

"Behold God beholding you … and smiling."
—Anthony de Mello, *Hearts on Fire: Praying With Jesuits*

"We are each a living manifestation of divinity. To know our self is to know God. So next time you pray for something do it with the knowledge that the answers lie within."
—Micheal Teal, *The Ancient One*

REFLECTION

Have you longed for God when you were broken and needed His guidance? Have you prayed and asked for His wisdom so you may understand? Did God grant it to you?

Have you struggled with thoughts or people who seem to intentionally diminish you? Have you ever felt God was protecting you or fighting for you because you couldn't fight any longer? If you were too weak and gave up the fight, what was the outcome?

My Blessed Angel

My dearest Aunt Sally,

You are my blessed angel! You have spoken words of encouragement and given me hope. You have helped me endure and hold on during times of spiritual warfare, especially when I felt defeated.

You have been generous and gracious, giving of yourself, as well as your treasured gifts, even if only on loan. You have offered all you possibly could to those in need, sacrificing and giving from your own need to help them, and never once have you ever expected anything in return.

You have understood me and known what to say. You have helped ease the turmoil and loss that has grieved me. You have given me courage and assured me, "Everything is going to be all right!"

You have understood my pain and heartache like God understands, with an unconditional loving and nonjudgmental heart. You have eased my agony and have truly blessed me when we have had our heart-and-soul talks.

You have always trusted others' sincerity when they came seeking you, whatever their needs. You have continued to pray for all people in need to be truthful. For those who are not in need, you have always hoped they would be completely honest with you, too.

You have battles of your own, but you still love deeply in spite of them. You have shared your stories, given true testimony, and passed on your legacy. You have hoped others will learn from your experience, generosity, and compassionate heart. You have tried to spare others the same pain and heartache you have experienced. You have always wanted to make a difference in the lives of God's people.

You have wanted people to remember and believe, with as much conviction as you, that each one of us can make a difference in someone's life. You have always hoped others will be blessed in ways that prove God is loving and merciful, and He lives in you!

You have touched people with a tender and humble heart through acts of kindness and true, unconditional love. You have loved me, just as I am; you have blessed me, just as you are! Always believing there is hope for a better tomorrow, you have moved my soul. You have made me want to be a better, loving Christian.

You have been a blessing and living sign of Christ among us! Commanded by Jesus, you have followed through. You have loved your neighbor, you have asked and received, you have sought and found whatever you needed to meet someone else's need!

Since you have survived similar depths of great pain and sadness like I have shared with you, you have helped guide me when I felt forsaken and defeated. You have helped me see this life is a battle I cannot survive on my own. You have explained and shown me how important it is to reach out, especially when I am discouraged and think I am not going to make it! You have taught me to seek and help others, "Because this is how we will survive!" Together, we have blessed, encouraged, and saved each other!

You have shown me what can be accomplished when we take time to help others. When we make time for what is important, we follow and answer God's calling in our lives!

When I felt I had too much to do and not enough time to do it, you tried to tell me I needed to surrender. You told me God would grant me enough time for what was important and what was necessary! I couldn't grasp the entire concept, but you have shown me how to share my time for the glory of our loving God!

Thank you for making time for me and being Christ in my life. May I be able to love others like you have loved me.

Eternally grateful, Connie

"There are no mistakes. The events we bring upon ourselves, no matter how unpleasant, are necessary in order to learn what we need to learn; whatever steps we take, they're necessary to reach the places we've chosen to go."

—Richard Bach, *The Bridge Across Forever*

"Never deprive anyone of hope ... it might be all they have."

—H. Jackson Brown, Jr., *Life's Little Instruction Book*

"And think not, you can direct the course of love; for love, if it finds you worthy, directs your course."

—Khalil Gibran, *The Prophet*

"If we live our lives as a gift, it is possible to reach a blissful state of eternal happiness. It is those who live their life with a sense of entitlement that undermine peace, freedom and liberty. Know that every breath is a miracle and every moment a blessing, and you will achieve your dreams."

—Micheal Teal, *The Ancient One*

REFLECTION

Aunt Sally Pasque was "My Blessed Angel." She helped me understand my heartache and gave me hope. She wept with me, because she felt the depth of my pain and agony. She prayed over me to protect me from Satan and his followers, and she was never judgmental. She loved me like only a mother can, just as I was, as if I was one of her own! This was one of the most God-like qualities she had, and she always made me feel special and loved.

God gave her stories to tell and an incredible wit and humor that was contagious, passing her gift onto her children. We laughed at some of the silliest things, sometimes we laughed till we cried. We could talk for hours, even when we only had a minute to stay, and she always wished we could spend more time together. She was a survivor in many ways. Speaking from her own experience, she was always able to encourage me!

God blessed Aunt Sally with worldly wisdom and empathetic eagerness to respond to the needs of others. She founded Compassionate Hearts to help those who were less fortunate. One of her most endearing wishes: "I never want anyone to think no one cares about them, or they have nowhere to turn. I never want someone to feel as though they have been abandoned."

Aunt Sally worked incredibly hard, whether people she helped ever realized her commitment. She always had compassion for people who came before her, regardless of their current struggle or joy. She always found something good in others and made a difference in people's lives by being someone who truly cared about each and every one of them. She was thoughtful, gracious, and sincere. She lived as Jesus commanded: *"Love one another as I have loved you!"*

Do you recognize the face of God or the face of an angel in people you've known for a long time or recently met? What is it about them that makes you believe they are Heaven sent?

Like Job, has your faith been tested? Have you ever felt as though you lost everything? Have you survived or recovered? If not, do you still believe?

I Am Not Alone

As I sat alone in silence, evening fell and darkness surrounded me; and yet, I was not alone. I felt God's presence around me, and in my still and quiet moments, I heard Him whispering my name ever so softly. He spoke to comfort and console me, saying, *"You are not alone; I am with you! I am here because I love you. I long for you to always be with Me."*

As I listened to His words of guidance and direction, He showed me His purpose for my life. I vowed a New Covenant to commit my life to live according to His plans for me.

With that, He took my hand and led me into the light. He walked with me on His paths of righteousness. By my side, He nurtured my soul with kindness and sheltered me from harm. He was gentle and tender at heart, loving me like no one on Earth!

I know God is my Father, my Lord and Savior, my hope for salvation! Truly blessed within His presence, I knew I was not alone.

"Live more mindfully, write a new chapter in your life, reclaim your wholeness and feel reverence in your heart, for by planting these seeds you will create a beautiful garden that will bear fruit to sustain your soul and nourish your spirit for eternity."
—Micheal Teal, *The Ancient One*

REFLECTION

My friend had recently become a widow, telling me her time alone was not alone. Sometimes she felt her husband's presence, but God was always with her. This feeling eased her grief and helped her transition to a new life without him. She enlightened me and helped me realize that even after the death of someone you love so much, they were still very close in spirit.

After the death of someone very dear to you, have you been blessed with subtle reminders and assurance, knowing you were going to be okay? Did you feel God was with you and you were not alone?

In the Breeze

In the breeze, I felt God's presence surround me—encircling me with His blessings and amazing grace. I accepted His kindhearted gesture, I believed in His sincere love, and I knew His concern for me was genuine. Acknowledging Him, I smiled and bowed my head in reverence. I was humbled by His wondrous existence and the difference He has made in my life.

In a nurturing way, He whispered and reminded me, *"Breathe. Listen to My Word and accept My promises for your life. Trust in Me. I am your hope and your salvation. Do not be afraid. I will grant you wisdom and understanding, peace and contentment, courage and perseverance to endure whatever comes your way. I will be the light on your path to lead you and guide you all the days of your life. If you continue to believe in Me, accept and follow My ways, you will spend Eternity with Me."*

I paused to contemplate what God had just shared with me. I felt completely suspended in that moment of consciousness, and time stood still.

Shifting the breeze slightly, God redirected my thoughts. He shared His hopes for me with glimpses of my future here and Heaven thereafter. He revealed things He wanted me to see and remember, even the place He has prepared for me in His Kingdom. He wanted to give me hope and a vision I could hang onto!

It seemed quite awhile before God spoke again, reminding me, *"You still need to breathe! You have come so far, and I see you are finally ready to put your total trust in Me, to let go of your past and current circumstances that have been holding you back. Reliving your daily torment has held you captive, denying you the ability to move forward. I command you to release the darkness and overpowering burdens that have compromised your peace of mind!*

"I forgave you so many years ago, yet you need to forgive yourself again. I have cleansed your heart, and I will not allow you to take back any of your past. Let it all go and leave it behind you. I need this newly acquired space in your life to make room in your heart to totally accept My unconditional love for you. I am granting you every bit of strength and encouragement you need to move forward in your life. You are worthy of this chance to believe! Let go and move on!

"Breathe in My purity! Exhale everything you need to surrender! As long as you continue to pray and remain in My presence, I will remain within your heart and soul. Once you finally surrender it all and place absolute trust in Me, I will fulfill and satisfy your longing to feel loved. Your world here will take on many changes, and you will be making significant adjustments in your life. Don't hold yourself back. You know this is what you need to do!"

God continued, hoping I would no longer question Him. *"I have already shown you what I have in store for your future. Accept this moment with Me as a gift you are worthy of receiving. Do not question My motives. I have only your best interests at heart."*

A sudden gust of wind broke my focus and God's Earthly presence immediately left me. Almost breathless at that moment, I sighed as I pondered what God had just told me.

Since 1986, God has indeed remained in my presence, whether I was aware or not. He has sustained my desire for life by providing me a measure of His strength, enough so I can endure and survive. He has fed my hunger for relationship, and He has continued to nourish my yearning heart and soul. He still blesses me more than I think I deserve, and He overwhelmingly calms my anxiousness with His gifts of peace and contentment.

Through all of my trials, struggles, and darkness, I have learned that whether a breeze is gentle and refreshing or mighty and powerful, I still believe in His promises, and I trust my heart and soul with Him.

⌣

"Although you have not seen him you love him; even though you do not see him now yet believe in him, you rejoice with an indescribable and glorious joy, as you attain the goal of your faith, the salvation of your souls."

—I Peter 1:8–9

"When you see Jesus as your Treasure, the Spirit has blown through your heart. Your joy in Jesus is a gift."

—John Piper, *When I Don't Desire God: How To Fight For Joy*

REFLECTION

A dear friend gave me the book *One Thousand Gifts: A Dare to Live Fully Right Where You Are* by Ann Voskamp—"A celebration of grace and recognition of the power of gratitude." The author had logged one thousand "gifts" that she acknowledged were from God. Within a few days, I had logged over one thousand gifts.

Write your own list of gifts and gratitude; include the times when you knew you were experiencing God's hand in your life. Whether it is something you have acquired or someone you love, it is a gift if He created it for you. He wants you to see His beauty and feel His presence and love. Give Him thanks, praise His Name, and you will be blessed abundantly!

What are you thankful for today?

A Message from God

God keeps trying to tell me ... why don't I want to hear?
Why don't I listen? What do I fear?
My heart is torn, my mind confused, I know not what to do,
though I find I must be learning, the answer is in You!

Why do I refuse to see the actions I must take?
Why can't I just let it go? Believe in God—He will not forsake!
Unsettled, stirred emotions, like wind blowing through my mind,
tangle my security, which I've longed for quite some time.

My desperate, searching heart longs to understand my soul,
seeking answers to my questions, and the secret God beholds.
Understanding heartache, God knows the pain I bear.
Forgiveness and unending love, His grace is always there!

Simple hidden messages in His presence, I do find
the beginning of my answers to the questions in my mind.
God keeps trying to tell me the secret of my soul ...
"Though your burdens may be heavy, trust Me, and let them go!

"I'll take the cross you're bearing, all your pain and brokenness ...
I control all life's storms—I calm ... I heal ... I bless!
So call upon Me always! Ask Me, and soon you'll find,
I am the answer you've been seeking, and I have been here all the time!"

"It is our part to seek, His to grant what we ask; ours to make a beginning, His to bring it to completion; ours to offer what we can, His to finish what we cannot."

—Saint Jerome, www.faithalive.com

"You don't learn by having faith. You learn by questioning, by challenging, by re-examining everything you've ever believed. And yet, all this is a matter of faith—the faith that there is a truth to be found. It is another paradox: To truly question, you must truly have faith."

—Tzvi Freeman, *Faithful Questions*

REFLECTION

Has God been sending you messages? Are you listening? What is He asking or telling you to do? Is something holding you back from doing what He has asked you to do, or what you know you should do?

Have you ever felt stuck, as though you knew what to do but you couldn't seem to follow through? Have you felt as though God was waiting for you to cry out and ask Him to help you, but you didn't feel worthy enough to ask? Did you believe God would help you if it were according to His will?

PART SEVEN

End of Life

"Take me home to your dwelling place
In your sweet embrace
ready to hold me in your arms.
Take me home to your loving eyes
With you alone, I'll rise singing forever,
In your arms, take me home."

DAVID HAAS, *Take Me Home*

Listening to God

Barely surviving, I realized I had been lost and wandering for a very long time. A wave of urgency suddenly forced me to find myself—to sink or swim—but I couldn't remember how to swim! I knew I needed to leave behind the darkness, but I didn't have any sense of direction. I didn't know how I would ever find my way back, yet I held onto a glimmer of hope that God would come and rescue me.

I managed to find enough strength to pray, and I focused all of my energy on listening for someone to enter my presence. God heard my prayer and immediately came before me. He assured me He would guide my way and lead me back to wholeness. *"I have been waiting for you, but I would have waited forever! I have always believed a day would come and you would seek Me, a day you would walk with Me and stand by My side."* Then, He urged me, saying, *"Trust Me! Just trust Me!"*

As we slowly made our way through a narrow passage, I tried to follow in His footsteps, but my weakened body kept wavering and missing His path. He spoke again, saying, *"You must still trust Me."* At that, He lifted me up and carried me. *"You will need your strength, so rest in My arms. I will remain with you even after we return. Trust that I will meet your every need. All you need to do is stay focused on Me."*

In the immediate moments that followed, God restored my spirit, overflowed my heart with His love, and nourished my soul with His presence. He cleared depression from my mind, turned my thoughts to hope and opportunity for a life of happiness and joy. He gave my body strength to endure my journey back to full health. His compassion and concern for my well-being fueled my ability to withstand and tolerate roadblocks, enabling me to return to a stable mental and physical condition.

During my recovery time with God, He reintroduced music in my mind, knowing I had forgotten how important it was for my soul. With His loving encouragement, God implanted a newfound respect for song and an awaking awareness in my heart to sing for His glory.

God acknowledged my hunger for spiritual growth, and I began to read books on the lives of saints. I attend Christian concerts, conferences, and missions to increase my faith. Planting me in the midst of people living and doing His work, God has shown me Christ lives within all of His people—in the midst of the poor, wounded, and brokenhearted, and in the bodies and souls of everyday people.

God has encouraged me to share His story of Mercy, to be an example of His love by showing His Spirit lives within me. He continues to be present in my daily life, and He inspires me to write and share my story with others. He smiles and reminds me how much He still loves me.

"I am honored you have chosen to follow Me and be My disciple. When you called Me from the depths of your darkness, I prayed you would thrive once again. Your courage and faith have saved you from the abyss, and I know you do believe and trust in Me. I am pleased with your commitment and dedication to walk with Me. The fullness of My love has been granted to you, and I bless you and your family. In the name of the Father, and the Son, and the Holy Spirit. Amen.

"Welcome back! Welcome Home!"

"All happenings, great and small, are parables whereby God speaks. The art of life is to get the message. To see all that is offered us at the windows of the soul, and to reach out and receive what is offered, this is the art of living."

—Malcolm Muggeridge,
The Very Best of Malcolm Muggeridge, Ian Hunter, Editor

"Man's advice cannot alleviate a troubled soul! When I'm really hurting, suffering deeply, I want to talk to some ordinary, unknown saint who has suffered heavily, and yet has come through it all praising God, comforted and full of faith! I want someone who has been tested in the fires of affliction—one who has known loneliness, sadness, sorrow, rejection, heartache. I want someone who has been to the point of giving up—and yet has trusted God and come forth rejoicing, believing, stronger than ever. They know the sympathy of Jesus, because His voice speaks true comfort to them in their hour of darkness. These sufferers become rich in spiritual resources. They develop a confidence born out of having endured tribulations and testings. Best of all, God gives them an influence they could not have gotten in any other way!"

—David Wilkerson, *World Challenge Pulpit Series*,
"The Suffering of Saints," September 26, 1994

REFLECTION

Is your life all you ever hoped it would be or is it lacking? If you think it is lacking, what are you willing to do? Are you ready to turn your life around?

If you have turned away from God, or simply have lost your way, have you tried to call out to Him? Are you ready to turn back and seek God?

Remember My Life

(In memory of my cousin Nels J. Northup)

God came and saved my life one day,
He adored me as His own.
It was then I promised to live in faith
and to follow Him thereon.

He delivered my heart from darkness,
led me away from Satan's harm.
He assured me if I believed in Him,
one day He'd take me Home.

God's forgiveness redeemed within my heart
His gracious and true love,
then He granted me a loving wife
to share His blessings from above.

Married, we raised a family;
in love, we taught them right from wrong.
We brought them up to worship God;
within, our faith was strong.

A wonderful life God gave to us,
and my promise to Him was kept.
Though my health had begun to fail,
I knew my life was blessed!

I was grateful for your presence;
in my thoughts, pain came and went.
Talking, listening, and sharing,
we knew my blessings were Heaven sent.

Thanks to all who prayed for me,
those who prayed right by my side.
You helped me stay focused …
in God's presence, you helped pass time.

God granted me His gift of strength
to persevere through night and day.
He stood beside me to the end
when my time here slipped away.

Though I know you thought I suffered,
my faith was strong in Him.
My days with you were blessings
and one day closer to Him.

I knew the affliction and pain I endured
would purify my soul.
In fear, I thought I'd not survive,
but now, just look, I am whole!

God's passion for love and mercy
blessed my soul all through my days.
Remember my life and thank God above,
giving Him all glory and praise!

"To touch the soul of another human being is to walk on holy ground."
—Stephen R. Covey,
The Wisdom and Teachings of Stephen R. Covey

"Love begins by taking care of the closest ones—the ones at home."
—Mother Teresa

REFLECTION

In 1958, Nels Northup married my cousin Linda Bricker. Together, they raised three daughters. Linda passed away with cancer in 1998. In 1999, Nels married Louisa Taylor, and they lived until "death do us part" in 2014. He was a loving husband and incredible father, a brother, coach, teacher, and mentor.

Nels was a man of God. He was loved, respected, and shared his wisdom. He increased one's self-confidence, and people enjoyed being around him.

Nels and I talked about love, marriage, and family values, and I cherished our time together. During his Memorial Service and Celebration of Life, I was honored and filled with pride listening to his pastor, family, friends, coaches, colleagues, and students share their stories and memories of someone they all loved so much.

May you also receive blessings that will change your life and the lives of others. Strive to be the type of person who makes a positive influence in the lives of people you meet every day!

How could you or do you make a difference in others' lives? Do you live every day with intention? Do you have a loving influence on the people you meet? Why or why not?

Passing of Time

(In memory of my neighbor John Looze)

My antique clock ticks away through the night;
my body is so tired, my eyes hurt inside.
I have cried many tears and cleansed my heart
while thinking of your family in this night that is so dark.

Through nighttime twilight outside my door,
I can see no one is home.
They are with you at the hospital, until you come home.
While the moon through a cloud casts its light through my mind,
I know doctors and nurses help you fight for more time.

For now, I keep vigil, all day and all night,
still hoping and wondering if you are really all right.
And as time evolves and brings forth each new day,
you are kept in my heart and my thoughts as I pray.

I ask for His peace in your innermost soul,
for God's love and promise and the grace He beholds.
Remember me, too, as I look out in the night,
may I find myself happy and ready for *new life*!

"Nothing can be sadder or more profound than to see a thousand things for the first and last time. To journey is to be born and die each minute. All the elements of life are in constant flight from us, with darkness and clarity intermingled, the vision and the eclipse; we look and hasten, reaching out our hands to clutch; every happening is a bend in the road … and suddenly we have grown old. We have a sense of shock and gathering darkness; ahead is a black doorway; the life that bore us is a flagging horse, and a veiled stranger is waiting in the shadows to unharness us."
—Victor Hugo, *Les Misérables*

REFLECTION

Pausing at my doorway before going to bed in the early morning hours, I looked out toward our neighbor's home. I felt a gnawing sense of loneliness while I gazed into the darkness, knowing John was in the hospital again. I knew his wife and children were keeping vigil through the night so he was not alone. I prayed for his family, but mostly for John:

"May God's presence calm your fear and ease your pain and suffering. May the touch of God's hand tenderly assure you it's going to be okay. I've been told and read that Heaven is wonderful, and God will wait until you are ready to accept your *New Life* with Him and everyone else who has gone before you. Even though you are afraid, you need to go and prepare a place for Sally and your family. Her turn will come one day, and before you know it, she will join you, and all this grief and heartache will have disappeared.

"In Heaven, time does not pass. It is all about living in the moment and being gloriously content and fulfilled. I know in my heart, God has found favor with you. May your peace come like the coolness of an evening breeze; and may your journey be swift, amazing, and a blessing beyond your wildest imagining. May this be a good and restful night for all of you!"

If you are nearing the end of your life, what do you wish or pray for yourself? Is there anyone you want to talk with before you pass away? What has kept you from meeting with them? What holds you back?

Have you had the opportunity to talk intimately with anyone who is dying? Have they shared what they fear or what they have questions about? If so, what were or are their concerns? If you have already experienced the opportunity, what did you learn that you didn't already know?

If someone you love is nearing the end of his or her life, what do you wish or pray for them?

God's Promise

(In memory of my neighbor Sally Looze, John's wife)

In the light, Jesus came for me; He took me by the hand.
He calmed my fear of passing on; He was gentle and so kind.
As we continued down the path, stopping sometimes to rest,
"You'll be healed forever! God's called you Home, at last!"

Heaven rejoiced when Jesus announced, *"Another has arrived!"*
They welcomed me with open arms; Jesus stood right by my side.
Unimaginable beauty and overwhelming love surrounds me here.
I cried with tears of thankful joy that God had Jesus bring me here!

And then, at last, I heard Dad's voice when he called out to me,
"Hey, Mama, I'm here and waiting! God promised us Eternity!"

"Do you seek a support more sure than the Word of God, which
is infallible? Surely, He has made the promise, He has written it,
He has pledged His word for it, it is most certain."
—Saint Augustine, *The Virtue of Confidence*

REFLECTION

"God's Promise" was a vision God granted me, allowing me to be present when Sally arrived in Heaven! I witnessed her smile with tears of joy when she saw her husband for the first time. With his beaming smile, I heard him call out to her, *"Hey, Mama!"* It was like music to her ears.

I marveled as they embraced and danced on into the evening like they always had. She was finally home and they both knew, without a doubt, Eternity was worth waiting for.

Have you wondered who might be waiting to meet you when you pass from this world to the next? Is there someone in particular whose voice you long to hear? Have you ever wondered or envisioned what it will be like when you hear their voice for the first time? Have you ever wondered what they might say to you or what you will say to them?

Mothering

(In memory of my mom, Darlene Cremeans Bricker Persons)

Our mother is mindful of meeting others' needs.
She offers love and affection;
she shows tenderness and teaches us right from wrong.

Our mother is a homemaker and makes our house a home.
Everything she does, she does for her family—
an extension of herself and her husband.

We must always be thankful and remember our mother
and all she has given us, all she has sacrificed in raising us.
By her instinct, she is nurturing and never seems to fail us.

Our mother is God's blessing for our family.

"One day you will ask me which is more important, my life or yours? I will say mine and you will walk away not knowing that you are my life."
—Khalil Gibran

"Life is a spiritual practice of blessings and inspiration where the seeds of loving kindness within our soul will blossom if we tend to them properly. Love is life's water, sprinkle it over your garden and a tree of life will grow that will bear fruit for eternity."
—Micheal Teal, *The Ancient One*

REFLECTION

I wrote "Mothering" for Mom on Mother's Day twenty years ago. It was during the final steps of completing my first book when Mom died suddenly. Pondering my life with her, I was grateful for our relationship and how much she loved all of us.

Mom was all about family—unconditional, true love and sacrifice. She was blessed with a heart and soul that thought of others before herself, and she taught us girls how to be wives, mothers, and grandmothers. She taught us about friendship and sharing, spending time together, and helping others whenever there was a need.

Mom taught us to communicate and stand up for what we believed. She taught us to work hard and work things out, to be honest and trustworthy, and the importance of respecting our husbands.

Mom was the kind of mother I wanted to be! She never complained about not having enough time, and she seemed to have her life and priorities in perfect order. She lived her life for others, especially for Dad, and had a gift of staying connected with her family and friends. She never forgot a birthday or anniversary. She always sent her homemade cards with a little note showing how much she loved every one of us!

Mom called us as much to share exciting news as to ask how everyone was. She always expected us to let her know when another baby was on the way and when another great-grandchild had arrived!

Two days before Mom passed, we spoke for the last time. She was calling to tell us how excited she was that our cousin Curt Bricker wanted to get together the following week. We talked about the birth of my ninth grandchild just a few days before. Though she didn't get to see her newest babies, she was proud to add another two great-grandsons to her count, and three more babies were on the way. She exuded love and pride in her twenty-six grandchildren, and forty-two great-grandchildren! What a legacy it was for her!

When I think of Mom and how much I miss her, I'm only a little sad, because she was reunited with Dad and so many family and friends. She was where she truly wanted to be. Mom's life was finally complete … she lived well, loved all of us well, and Dad welcomed her Home that very day. What a joy for both of them, and what a blessing for us that she was our mother and grandmother!

My Legacy

(In memory of my cousin Linda Bricker Northup)

It was early in the morning. Pure, fresh air from an open window above my pillow brushed across my un-blanketed skin. Outside, leaves on the trees at the edge of the woods remained nearly motionless. I heard the sound of silence; I felt the stillness in the air.

I lay awake in bed next to my loving husband. This unusual awakening was quiet and peaceful, clear and uncluttered, void of the rush of this world. I was exceptionally alert and ready for a new day.

Completely aware of my surroundings, I closed my eyes. As if frozen in time, I was barely breathing and perfectly still. Noticing my husband's effortless breathing in and out captured my attention, and I turned my head to gaze upon his silhouette on the wall beyond our bed. I observed "this man" God chose for me. I would have loved to wake him so he could share this rare moment with me, but I let him sleep. My consciousness soon shifted and focused on the rise and fall of my own chest. I thanked God for His breath of life within me, within both of us.

My thoughts shifted again, from God's breath of life to visions of life-giving blood flowing back and forth within my body. It was accompanied by distinct sensations of life within me. I heard my pulse echo from my pillowcase; I felt a pulsating rhythm with each additional heartbeat, envisioning my heart tirelessly at work sustaining my existence in this moment. With a grateful heart, I thanked God for this extraordinary feeling and consciousness I was being blessed with. I thanked Him for allowing me additional time to comprehend and acknowledge "who I am." I thanked Him for granting me contentment in these moments of peacefulness.

Like a soft blink of light from a firefly, I realized God was in my midst! His presence surrounded me with tenderness and soothed away all of my fatigue, pain, and earthly cares. He led my thoughts when I closed my eyes again, overflowing my heart and soul with His grace. He lovingly directed memories of my past, allowing me to look back and see lessons I had needed to learn. He also showed me glimpses of what He wanted me to look forward to, so I would no longer be afraid of what was to come.

God's presence reassured me, promising me He would always remain by my side. His kindness and unconditional love would continue through Eternity to fill my soul, and then He magnified my ability to comprehend His boundless affection for me. He granted me His holy gift of understanding and showed me His divine purpose for my life. He firmly and compassionately commanded me to trust in His wisdom and accept His love for me; in return, I was to share it with others.

God led me and I followed Him, pondering everything I saw. Occasionally pausing, He showered me with additional compassion beyond my understanding. Captivated by all that encompassed me, He allowed me additional moments to appreciate His immensity. He watched over my amazement and observed my astonishment as I truly began to comprehend how almighty and powerful He truly was! He granted me a renewed gift of love and He cleansed my soul. He opened my heart to receive His blessings, those I previously thought were not intended for me. He knew I still struggled sometimes feeling unworthy, sometimes unable to forgive myself for choices I had made. Sometimes, I still felt abandoned, but He loved me in spite of it.

God continued to walk with me through His majestic realm of Heaven, showing me the room He has prepared for me when my time comes. When He introduced me to everyone present, a huge smile overcame my state of contentment and tears streamed down my face. I realized moments like this with God were rare! It was an honor and a privilege He bestowed upon me to preview all His radiant beauty and love, to be granted the opportunity to see life ever after.

When He spoke to me, He repeated what He had told me numerous times before, just making sure I knew, believed, and still remembered.

"This is what you have to look forward to—everlasting love and Everlasting Life with Me and those you love most deeply. This is Eternity, and I have promised it to you, forever and ever."

My soul was overjoyed, and His love radiated within me. His grace and peace gladdened my heart, lifting my spirits higher than ever before. Granting me His gift of eternal hope, He removed all fear and apprehension.

As I stood in God's Heavenly Kingdom, I was speechless and breathless in awe of such beauty until my husband stirred beside me, but God instantly called me back to Him. Once again, we were together in Heaven, in the stillness of that moment. Before slowly bringing me back to reality of this world, God comforted me and freed me from all worries. He calmed my thoughts and prayed with me. Embraced in His arms, with His kind and gentle voice, He spoke words of hope and inspiration.

"May you comprehend and accept the fullness of My love and the love of others. Share My love and joy. Share all that fills your soul with wonder and happiness—share all My gifts that make you who you are.

"Tell your story. Share your experience with others. Show them what makes your heart move with compassion and understanding. May your journey be a true sign of My incredible love! I will hold this as one of your greatest blessings! May all who love you do the same!"

I inhaled deeply, exhaled slowly, and quietly drifted off.

"What you leave behind is not what is engraved in stone monuments, but what is woven into the lives of others."
—Pericles, *Prince of Tyre*

"Jesus teaches us another way: Go out. Go out and share your testimony, go out and interact with your brothers, go out and share, go out and ask. Become the Word in body as well as spirit."

—Pope Francis

REFLECTION

"My Legacy" was written during a very trying time of my life. It evolved from my relationship, love, and close bond with my cousin Linda Bricker Northup while she was dying of cancer. She was quite a bit older than me, but our lives, from time to time, seemed very much the same—our husbands loved us deeply, more than we thought we deserved, and we loved our families.

Linda and I shared our stories, described our struggles within our minds and souls. We talked about simple things, but when we believed in something, we both had an incredible passion for it. We believed in love, commitment, and the importance of strong family values. We were grateful for things we were fortunate enough to accomplish and wept over things we knew we would miss … watching our grandchildren grow, being available for our children, and continuing our lives with our loving husbands. We expressed our hopes and what we wanted to be able to witness and experience in this lifetime. In the end, we had no regrets, and we both commented, "I am ready whenever God calls me Home!"

This book is my legacy … my gift from God to you! May you be blessed and given the opportunity to share your legacy, too!

If you knew your death was near, could you define your legacy? Has it been revealed to you? What would you want people to know or remember about you?

How well do you know your relatives and dearest friends? Do you know them well enough to be able to share their legacy with others or with the next generation? How would you pass their legacy on?

More Than Just a Visit

It was a peaceful morning in June 1986. I had completed videotaping a newborn moments after birth, and I was now headed to the country home I grew up in. I felt as though I was on a journey between two worlds: from God's miracle of birth and newborn life to my parents' home where Dad was dying of cancer, awaiting his imminent death.

Exhilaration began to waver as my thoughts shifted and my heart sank. I realized this would be Dad's last Father's Day. Immediately, overwhelming grief and heartache swept over me; I sobbed, nearly blinded by my tears and thought, what am I going to get Dad for Father's Day?

And then, God spoke to me for the first time. *"You are my dad!"* The phrase echoed a few times in my mind before I pulled off the road and began to write: "You are my dad, and I love you so!" Within a few brief moments, "You Are My Dad" was complete (see page 170); it said exactly what I needed to say. I pondered what I had written for a moment, and then drove the rest of the way to Mom and Dad's.

My unexpected visit gave Mom a bit of relief, so I decided to stay for a while before going home. It was just the three of us—Mom, Dad, and me. I sat at the foot of their bed, talking while Mom came and went from their bedroom. Dad and I conversed like never before.

Dad talked about the day I was born, telling me, "You were a cute baby" and how much he loved every one of us. We divulged what we loved about each other, and what made us happy and proud. We talked about what disappointed us and let us down, as well as who and what broke our hearts. We shared what we knew was important to our family. Dad reminisced about our family trip to Florida with Mom and all six of us kids in a station wagon. He chuckled when he said, "Wouldn't Bill be surprised if we all drove in today!"

At times, intensity in our voices rose, and we laughed aloud; then, as if out of nowhere, in a moment of silence, we wept. Lumps in our throats, barely able to speak, we still said what we wanted to say. I realized this was the only time I ever saw Dad cry.

TWENTY-FIVE YEARS LATER

Time has passed since that day, but out of nowhere, once again I was overcome with sadness. I was caught off-guard by the pendulum's unexpected sweep of grief, as intense as it was back then. Caught in an undertow of tears, I simply sobbed and let them go, allowing them to cascade down my face.

In my mind, I vividly saw Dad lying on his bed, a strong man weakened by cancer in a very short time; I saw him sitting in his lawn chair, unable to keep warm in the heat of that summer; I saw his agony when his pain was out of control; I saw his inner struggle before he talked to Reverend Henry Alexander; I saw him lying in his hospital bed, barely able to communicate; I saw how sad we were and our concern for Mom, wondering how she was going to survive the loss of her first and only true love, wondering how Uncle Bill and all of my brothers and sisters were going to survive, wondering how I was going to survive.

Looking back over the years that followed, I was still acknowledging the magnitude of my pain, finally being able to recognize and piece together the long-term effects of Dad's and Uncle Bill's deaths. I observed how my overwhelming grief took away my health in 1987, and I watched my body and brain shut down. I flashed back to my struggle—body, mind, and soul—seeing how long it took for me to recover. I saw how my inability to process grief and sorrow changed my life more than anyone could have ever imagined. At this point in time, none of us were able to realize how much we would still miss him to this day.

Overcome by this immediate vacuum of emotion, I continued to cry. I could see and feel the expanse of my great sadness. I already knew how quickly it consumed me, and I realized how vulnerable I still am. Before I saw it coming, I was "stuck in time," as if it had all happened yesterday.

The very next moment, God spoke, re-directed my thoughts, and calmed me in His presence. *"Take a deep breath! You know you must shake off your sad thoughts. It's too easy for you to slip back into this side of your memory and devastating loss. Only I can banish your feelings of despondency, slow your tears, and continue to encourage you.*

"In this moment with Me, take another deep breath! Consciously turn your thoughts to see the good times you remember with your dad! Look into his eyes and see the pride on his face; see his smile and listen to him laugh; see the depths of love he had for all of you and how much he loved your mom; listen to his voice when he speaks and remember what you learned from him being your dad."

Pausing for a moment, I took several more intentional deep breaths, and I followed God's direction. He knew exactly what I needed! I needed to hear His voice, and when He spoke, He knew I would listen to Him, just as I used to do with my dad.

As I transitioned my thoughts, I was instantly relieved, and I thanked God for our time together with Dad. I smiled and vividly saw how much I loved Dad and how much he loved every one of us. Repeatedly smiling, I sighed and realized I could breathe easily once again! Thanks be to God!

⌣⌢

"May the LORD give might to his people; may the LORD bless his people with peace!"

—Psalm 29:11

"Therefore, confess your sins to one another, and pray for one another, that you may be healed. The fervent prayer of a righteous person is very powerful."

—James 5:16

REFLECTION

No matter when our parents die, I have heard so many people say they have never gotten over their loss … and I agree. I still feel a great sadness and deep sense of loss.

Seek within yourself to find the words you need to express yourself. Share your feelings with those close to you so they will understand what you are going through. May you be blessed with God's gift of peace.

Have you recovered from the loss of the one you loved so dearly? Has time healed your pain? If so, what helped you move on from sadness to comforting joy? If not, would you consider talking to someone who could help facilitate your ability to process your grief? Have you ever considered Hospice Grief Recovery?

You Are My Dad

(In memory of my dad, Calvin E. Bricker)

You are my dad, and I love you so!
Though I seldom take the time
to tell you how I feel,
it does cross my mind.

You are my dad, and I am so proud!
Every time I think of you,
my tears just seem to flow,
and I know I'm going to miss you so!

You are my dad, but you are really so much more …
most important of all,
you are the husband to my mom,
the father, and grandfather of us all!

You are my dad, and we all love you so!
You and Mom have taught us all so much—
about pride, honesty, respect …
how two can love a lifetime
and love us all so much!

You are my dad, and even though you're gone,
we will never forget all the times that we shared;
we will keep you close until we all meet again.

You are my dad, and we all love you so!

REFLECTION

God's gift of writing and rhythms of poetry began the first day God spoke to me, *"You are my dad."* I clearly heard Him and He inspired me to write this first piece. What a blessing God gave me that day as each phrase came to me and echoed in my mind. With tears streaming down my face, I knew this was Dad's gift for Father's Day!

The End or The Beginning

I used to think all books began at the beginning and continued through to the end—but there is no end to this book if any part of my life experience has touched you. I hope this book has urged you to find your own answers or inspired you to continue the journey within yourself. I hope and pray you will be able to clarify what you believe and know where you are going, as well as find and experience your own love, peace, and joy … thus, *the beginning of a better life!*

Some people think life begins at birth; I believe your life began before you were conceived. God already had a plan when He chose your mother and father. Your mother began to know you when you moved within her womb; your parents may have named you before you were born; your family came to know you after your birth, when they could actually see you and hold you in their arms.

Every day is *a new beginning*, no matter what may have happened in the past, even if it was only yesterday. We must learn to be thankful for all things, whether we believe they are good or bad, there is always a lesson! Some people think death is the end of life, but I believe God has promised Eternal Life to those who believe and follow Him … thus, *the beginning of Everlasting Life!*

If you are not happy with the person you are, choose a *new beginning*! Seek God and ask for forgiveness; change your ways to Godly ways. He forgives you before you comprehend or regret what you have done. God's love and forgiveness is guaranteed; it is not conditional! He will wait as long as it takes for you to confess—until you are sorry and seek Him—until you humbly ask with an honest and sincere heart for His Mercy!

Seek forgiveness from those you have hurt—whether it was something you said or didn't say, whether it was a result of your actions or something you didn't do. If you walked away and you knew you should have stayed, ask them to forgive you when you are sorry. It is their choice to accept your sincerity and grant it to you, but don't be surprised if they are not able to forgive you at this time. If you are sincere and you say "I'm sorry," it may make a world of difference in someone's ability to forgive, especially if your sins are sins of the heart, especially when it is your family!

Forgive those who have hurt you, whether or not they say "I'm sorry." Accept the apology you may never receive. You can choose to forgive those who have trespassed against you, because it is your choice to release the bondage unforgiveness holds in your heart.

Lastly, forgive yourself! Sometimes this is the most difficult to achieve. God forgives you, others forgive you, so why is it so difficult to forgive yourself? If this is what is holding you back from living a *happier life*, pray for your own forgiveness. Once you can let go, God will replace what you have released with other blessings ... thus, *the beginning of a happier life!*

Accept His gracious gifts to fulfill your heart's desire, to live according to His will, and to return peace and joy in your life. May your journey lead you to the Promised Land, the Land of *Everlasting Life,* and to live with Him and those you love in Eternity!

⌒⌒

"... that there will come a time
when you believe everything is finished.
That will be the beginning."
—Louis L'Amour, *Lonely on the Mountain*

Afterword

By the time I finished writing this book, I had retired from my fulltime job, and I was spending more time with my family. I have loved and appreciated my husband more than I ever thought possible, and we have both forgiven each other more than we thought we ever could. I thank God for continuing to humble me and show me the significance of loving and forgiving others as He has forgiven me!

Each day I continue to be inspired by God's loving kindness and mercy. He has never lost hope in me, given up on me, or stopped believing in me. Through His loving and faithful people, I am surely blessed!

For those of you who continue to seek your own answers, may God grant you His wisdom and insight to comprehend and understand everything you still need to learn.

Be blessed on your journey!

About the Author

CONNIE BRICKER SHALER was born at home and grew up in the country near the Jordan River Valley in Northern Michigan. She is one of seven children raised on a farm. Her mom was a loving mother, devoted wife, and homemaker; her dad served in the U.S. Army and worked at East Jordan Iron Works until his diagnosis of cancer in 1986. A farmer at heart, he planted organic vegetable gardens, raised trophy Herford cattle, and was proud of his loving family. Connie's parents taught the importance of good work ethics and instilled strong moral values—love, honesty, and respect.

After graduating high school, Connie married Frank A. Shaler. They remain in the community where they both grew up and raised three children. They now have nine grandchildren.

Just before Connie's dad died in 1986, God spoke to her for the first time, and she began to write. In less than a year, she also grieved over the deaths of her uncle, aunt, cousin, and grandfather. In July 1987, her body shutdown and she was diagnosed with Chronic Fatigue Syndrome (CFS), unknown origin. In spite of continued grieving and the loss of her own health, her faith grew stronger. In 1995, she began to recover physically, regained some strength, but continued a battle within her soul. It was in December 2009 when she came to realize severe depression had caused her CFS.

Connie worked many years for Mark Patrick at State Farm Insurance with her younger sister, Bette. She loved her job and the people she worked with, but retired in 2014 to spend more time with her family and focus on completing her first book.

God granted Connie an amazing appreciation for music and used music to nurture her soul. She remains active in her faith community, sings, and plays flute in the church choir.

To this day, Connie still hears God's voice. She listens to His words of guidance and writes whenever He speaks and inspires her to write. She continues to struggle with major depressive episodes and Satan's warfare, but God protects her soul, helps her endure, and blesses her well.

The writings in this book reflect the author's struggle, survival, and ongoing recovery.

Contact the Author

Connie would like to hear from you. Please share your comments and thoughts to let her know how *A Voice of Hope* touched your life. She will respond to all inquiries.

If you would like to schedule a speaking engagement or book signing event in your area, please contact Shaler Publishing.

If you would like to receive notices of the author's upcoming books or a calendar of events, please include your email address.

You may contact Connie Bricker Shaler via her publisher:

Shaler Publishing
843 N. Advance Road
Boyne City, MI 49712
Email: connie@shalerpublishing.com
www.shalerpublishing.com

To order additional copies of this large-print edition, please visit the website above (paperback and hardcover editions also available online) or mail a note and payment of $32.50 per copy (includes 6% Michigan sales tax and shipping and handling) to the publisher.

Volume discounts are available.